When She Cries

Women of Alabaster

Nancy Hulshult

979-8-9935587-2-1

Published and Designed by:
NarratusCreative | NarratusPress | narratuscreative.com
P.O. Box 1413, Hamilton, OH 45012
Produced in the United States of America

All proceeds of this book support Women of Alabaster - thank you in advance!
To donate or to learn more: www.womenofalabaster.org
To schedule Scarlet Hudson and others for speaking engagements:
scarlet@womenofalabaster.org
To speak to Scarlet: 513-543-5656
To send donation by check written to "Women of Alabaster":
7716 Arlington Rd. Dillsboro, IN 47018

For other books written by Nancy Hulshult: www.nancyhulshult.com

DEDICATION

GIGI DURNELL WILSON
WOMEN OF ALABASTER VOLUNTEER

This book is dedicated to Gigi Durnell Wilson and the women who fought their battles until they could no more. Gigi was a light in the WOA Family. She dedicated several years to volunteering in the Day Center and Street Outreach. During our Covid shutdown, Gigi made prayer blankets to cover those at Christ Hospital who could not have family during their passing. Gigi put love into each blanket she made. The prayers said over those blankets touched not only the patients, but also their families after the loved one passed. She was a lover of the Lord and all His children. Gigi passed away on June 19, 2021. She is so missed and loved. Rest In Peace.

When She Cries

ACKNOWLEDGMENTS

Women of Alabaster Board of Directors

Ronda Croucher, Chairwoman of the Board of Directors for Women of Alabaster

About 10 years ago, I was first introduced to the dark truth that children and vulnerable women were being trafficked. It so grieved me that I joined with my cousin, Denise Chaney, who was working with an anti-trafficking group in Atlanta. We were traveling down there and working to support efforts there, and the director of that program challenged us to find out what was happening in our community. We did and realized that for all of the good work being done to help people, that Jesus needed to be part of the solution. That's when we met "Mama Scar." And the Lord sent her to Butler County. Today I have the privilege of serving on the Board of WOA. Scarlet is one of the most sincere, genuine and loving people I have ever known. She loves fiercely and fights for "her girls". Now she's training an army of warrior women to do the same, and I'm privileged to stand alongside her in this beautiful ministry.

Chris Witzgall, Treasurer and past Vice Chairman and Chairman of the Board of Directors for Women of Alabaster (8 years on board)

I am part of WOA because I have a heart for women who are exploited by evil people. I am blessed to use my God given gifts and talents to support the ministry, and love when the women find that Jesus is the ultimate healer to transform their lives.

Anita Ridener, Secretary of the Board of Directors for Women of Alabaster

I have long believed in the mission of Women of Alabaster. I have served Women of Alabaster in various ways, and each time it was impactful. It was during an outreach run that I truly understood why WOA must exist when I looked into the eyes of a frightened and hopeless woman. Her eyes told the story why WOA must do what they do. Someone must help her. Someone must point her toward hope. You can't unsee those eyes.

Ambrosia Jones, Board Member, Board of Directors for Women of Alabaster

As a board member, I am committed to the ministry's mission and believe in actively supporting it. By working collaboratively with the team, I aim to contribute to the successful operation of the ministry's organization.

Greg Howard, Chaplain for Women of Alabaster (8 years)

As Chaplain for Women of Alabaster, I feel it is a great honor and privilege to be able to pray for all those who work for the Ministry and for their families, but especially for the vulnerable women who have been trapped in sex trafficking and drug and alcohol addiction. I pray for their salvation, that they find Jesus and break free from the bondage they have been living in. I pray for them to be able to live the life that God has intended for them.

Women of Alabaster Community Partners

Amy Amann

My first exposure to Women of Alabaster was at my church. I would usually notice a woman with red hair sitting on the far left side of the sanctuary with two, three or several other women sitting with her and they called her "Mama Scar." I would later find out that her street name was given to her by the girls who were on the downtown streets of Cincinnati where she was serving..

It so happened that we had a mutual friend, Debby Shutte, and she said that she went out on the streets in Cincinnati with Scarlet and some other volunteers. She asked if I would like to go out one night to minister with them, and I jumped at the chance. I believed the Lord put it in my heart when I was very young to serve the brokenhearted.

From the moment I got out and prayed with the first woman, my heart was so full of compassion for these ladies, and I wanted to do more. After some time of serving on the sidelines, I felt the calling to ask Scarlet about my working with the ministry full time and was able to serve for almost two years before I was called back to other employment for personal and financial reasons.

Scarlet couldn't get rid of me that easily, and I still volunteer and plan to spend more time with the ministry again when I retire. This ministry is dear to my heart, and it means so much to me to be a part of the Women of Alabaster team! To the ladies we serve, "I love you more!"

Jesus said in Luke 4:18:

> *"'The Spirit of the Lord is upon Me, Because He has anointed Me to preach the gospel to the poor; He has sent Me to heal the brokenhearted, To proclaim liberty to the captives And recovery of sight to the blind, To set at liberty those who are oppressed.'"* NKJV

Pastor Cheryl Blackburn

There are moments in life when we are confronted with the undeniable reality of suffering: moments that compel us to act, to speak, and to stand in the gap for those who cannot fight for themselves. I met Scarlet Hudson in 2012, I accompanied her in ministry, and I grew to know her as the most unselfish person I have ever known. This book is born from her calling. It is a testament to the power of her faith, resilience, and the unwavering love of God in the face of unimaginable darkness. Scarlet Hudson, founder of Women of Alabaster, has walked along survivors, offering hope where there was once despair, bringing restoration and salvation to those the world has seemed to have forgotten. I have had the privilege of witnessing firsthand the impact of Women of Alabaster Ministry in seeing lives transformed, chains broken and futures rewritten through the power of God's love. Through relentless dedication, Scarlet and her ministry volunteers refuse to turn away from those in crisis. This ministry is a beacon of hope and a reminder to us all that no one is beyond redemption, and everyone is worth saving! This ministry goes into the dark places with the Light of our Lord Jesus Christ, and lives are changed!

Mary Kristi Brashear, MK Curated Tours, LLC
She Stands – a Watchman – a Door
In October 2023, Scarlet Hudson ventured to Israel with a group of friends. Our itinerary was to include nine days exploring the country, followed by several days learning about and participating in a ministry in Tel Aviv that serves those living on the streets.

Our adventure was abruptly interrupted by the outbreak of war on October 7, right in the middle of our trip. Sirens would blare, and everyone would rush to the bomb shelters. Once everyone was secure, we would find Scarlet standing at the door as a barrier, keeping watch and ensuring the safety of those who entered. She would then cover everyone in prayer.

When the bombings ceased, we would often find Scarlet, aka Mama Scar, lying prostrate on the chapel floor, worshiping, praying, and seeking the Lord's presence while interceding for the defenseless on the streets.

I liken our time in Israel to Scar's everyday life as the Founder and Director of Women of Alabaster. Every single day, she finds herself amid someone's battle. She positions herself to help others find safety. She pours the Word of God over them, enveloping them in prayer. She points the way to the Savior. She stands as a WATCHMAN and SERVES as a DOOR of escape and refuge.

Pastor John Calabrese, *LifeSpring Community Church*
The work of Women of Alabaster is a powerful testament to God's heart for the broken and His call to bring light into the darkest places. Scarlet Hudson's obedience to that call has not only transformed her life, but has also rescued and restored countless others trapped in the grip of trafficking and addiction. At LifeSpring, we are honored to partner with this ministry, standing alongside those who fight for freedom, healing, and hope. This book is more than a story— it is an invitation to witness God's relentless love at work.

Pastor Doug Combs, *Church on Fire*
Scarlet Hudson, affectionately known as Mama Scar, is an absolute hero to those

that know her. She has a love for the hurting and broken like very few I have ever met. She has the heart of a lion and has little fear when it comes to ministry in the streets.

It is said that the Lord will take your mess and make it your message. What a message Mama has: a message of hope, restoration and healing. She puts feet to her message. She gets in the trenches and loves the girls right out of their life of desperation.

The stories in this book will touch your heart and make you want to hit the streets. They are stories of lives changed through Jesus Christ and a woman called Mama Scar, a true hero and giant of the faith.

Pastor Wendell and Kim Coning, *Hamilton Dream Center*
Several years ago, we were told that we just had to meet this lady that had a women's street ministry in Cincinnati. As pastors of the Hamilton Dream Center in the inner city of Hamilton, we were a little skeptical, having met with so many other different ministries We set up a meeting, and in walks this red haired lady and begins to share her passionate heart about women on the streets who are often forgotten and abused. Scarlet Hudson is the real deal with a heart after God! Women of Alabaster is a well organized pattern for every ministry to model.

It is an honor to partner with Scarlet and Women of Alabaster, a ministry that is making a difference around the world!

Pastor Daniella Gibbons, *Hamilton Dream Center / Anna Hour Prayer*
Scarred and scared are the women who are more childlike than their appearances show. Battles fought in dark places from early ages caused by illegal touches, and harmful, generational acceptances which never protected the innocence of their youth. These hurtful, yet cultural norms of broken families, perversion and abuse can be found in the foundation of nearly every soul wandering the streets of our cities. The good news is that light shines brightest in the darkest places. There is hope. There is freedom.

The answer to the brokenness lies in a community of women who have overcome by the blood of The Lamb and by the word of their testimony.

On these pages, you will hear the stories of those hidden and forgotten in the shadows of sex trafficking, shared through the experiences and encounters of "Mama Scar," a beloved woman of faith and courage.

I urge you to allow your heart to be fully present in these events. Authorize the Spirit of The Lord to release a righteous roar for His justice, joined with the words and heart posture of Jesus Himself in Mark 14, *"Leave her alone."*

Pastor Brian Hoehler, *New Hope Community Church*
Scarlet Hudson is a beacon of hope and unwavering compassion in the Cincinnati community. As the founder and leader of Women of Alabaster, she has dedicated her life to helping women caught in the devastating cycles of sex trafficking and addiction. With tireless effort and a heart of service, Scarlet has provided these women with a path to healing and restoration, offering not just support, but the transformative power of faith. Through her ministry, she has introduced countless individuals to the life-changing beauty of Jesus Christ, empowering them to reclaim their worth and dignity, and embrace a future filled with hope and possibility.

Bob Hudson, husband of Scarlet Hudson
I know one thing. When we get to heaven, my wife will be driving a Rolls Royce, and I will be following behind her on a skateboard. The things that she has accomplished in life are remarkable, and I'm so happy to have her as my wife. She's a wonderful and beautiful, beautiful, beautiful soul, and she's all Godly in every way. I love you, Hon!

Lisa Johnson, Cincinnati Police Officer
The Women of Alabaster sometimes don't know the names of the women they help or the ones that come in for food and shelter, but they know that their help is needed and give it without question. That's why I love them and will always be here to help. They are all in.

Pastor Marti Landis, Founder, *Resilient Women's Ministry*
Women of Alabaster ministry is truly a beacon of hope and restoration, embodying Christ's love in action. Scarlet Hudson and her leadership team clearly have a deep commitment to serving others, not just in word, but in tangible ways that make a real difference. Ministries like this are such a testament to the power of faith and community in bringing healing and transformation. What an incredible mission!

Randy T. Rogers,
Secretary-Treasurer of the Religious Alliance Against Pornography and Retired Judge from Butler County, Ohio
"She never quits," are the words used by one prominent community leader in describing Scarlet Hudson. President Theodore Roosevelt once said, "Knowing what's right doesn't mean much unless you do what's right." Scarlet Hudson, or "Mama Scar" as she is known, is a person who does "what's right."

I came to know Scarlet Hudson just a couple of years ago while seeking information about local and regional efforts to meet the needs of persons harmed by sexual trafficking. My role at the time was that of a researcher for an organization I then helped to lead, seeking to discover what I could about the existence of sexual trafficking and its connection to the ever-increasing growth of pornography use in America.

I had arranged to meet Scarlet at the local outreach of a non-profit ministry she had formed years before, known as Women of Alabaster, Inc. To gain entrance to the location, I had to go to the slightly battered back door of an old church that was located a block away from the city's main thoroughfare. After I pushed a button, a friendly person unlocked and opened the metal door and ushered me down a seemingly endless set of steps that led to the basement of the old church. At the bottom of the steps I came to the entrance of a modestly decorated space that glowed with what I later understood to be the presence of kindness and compassion. After a brief tour of the facility, I sat down across the desk from this remarkable lady people call "Mama Scar."

It was then that I learned about how Scarlet Hudson, as a young woman had overcome her own set of personal challenges, and then, with very little education, went on to forge her own way near the top of her profession as a corporate trainer in the glamour industry. In that job, Scarlet taught others to teach women how to look better on their outside in hope of them feeling better on their inside.

The stories I heard that day were captivating. First, I heard about when Scarlet accompanied a friend from her church on a Friday night evangelistic excursion to minister to prostitutes walking the seedy streets of a large nearby city. She explained how her encounter with one pistol-whipped prostitute pried her away from her lucrative position in the world of glamour and the comfortable life she then enjoyed. Scarlet's new life involved regular visits to those seedy streets and multiple encounters with other used, abused, and forgotten women. Scarlet began to make friends with the friendless. "Women of Alabaster" emerged from those seedy streets, to "provide a pathway to freedom for vulnerable women who are victims of sex trafficking and addiction." Scarlet then told me about the hundreds of needy women who had since received food, comfort and care from Scarlet and the band of merry volunteers she was able to gather around her.

Scarlet Hudson once taught others to teach women how to look better on their outside. Through the Women of Alabaster ministry, Scarlet and her volunteers now show other women how to be better on their inside. I saw several such volunteers that first day I interviewed Scarlet. They effortlessly moved through that glowing space I discovered in that church basement, caring for one woman from the nearby streets to the next, asking, "Do you want something to eat?"

"Can I sit here with you?" "Do you need to take a shower?" "Can we get you some clean clothes?" "Do you know Jesus?" "Can I pray with you?"

It was a marvelous thing to watch them "do what's right."

Thank you, Mama Scar. I hope the Women of Alabaster never quit.

Heidi Roth
God is faithful. He will not let you be tempted beyond your ability, but with the temptation, He will also provide the way of escape that you may be able to endure it. - 1 Corinthians 10:13

This verse says a lot, and I am grateful for the impact Mama Scar and the Women of Alabaster have had on my recovery. The love these women show every day is a love I've never known until they came into my broken life with every prayer, every meal, and every hug. I began to see God working through them, and they never gave up on me, and that means so much to me. Thank you, Mama Scar and WOA. You have forever made an impact on my life, and I've never felt more close to God than I do right now. Forever grateful.

Judge Heather Russell, Hamilton County Municipal Court
I started the Drug Court/Human Trafficking Court called CHANGE Court (Changing Habits and Setting New Goals is Empowering) in 2014. One participant was always talking about Momma Scarlet. I thought Momma Scar was her biological mother, but soon learned that Scarlet was her spiritual mother.

Over these last 11 years, I have encountered so many prostituted women who see Scarlet as their spiritual mother. When a person has experienced repeated trauma, their bodies and spirits are broken. Their addiction is the strongest attraction they feel; however, with Scarlet's continuous presence, love, and spirituality, Scarlet is able to bring a great number of this most vulnerable group in from the streets, and she is then able to awaken their spirituality. It is quite breathtaking to see Scarlet involved in the baptism of women who were literally lost, and now Found.

Scarlet's work happens without government funding. Her urban buildings and her farm come from donors, who see Momma Scarlet as I do. Scarlet's faith is like love..not a material thing, but with Scarlet you can reach out and touch faith, touch the purest love, as the name of her farm, Agape, reminds us. I am of a different faith than Scarlet, but in these most difficult post October 7 times, she reaches me in ways that my own congregation does not, especially when she quotes Old Testament scripture in Hebrew and shares music from Jerusalem with me. I have personally seen and felt Scarlet's transformative work. She is a Proverbs 31 Woman of Valor. I am called "Your Honor," but it is I who hold the

Honor to tell you about Momma Scarlet.

Christopher E. C. Smitherman, Past Vice Mayor, City of Cincinnati
Women of Alabaster is a ministry that saves lives of women who have no way out of human trafficking. Women of Alabaster is the penicillin with GOD at the center. The women involved trust Women of Alabaster, and the community embraces its mission. This combination of trust and love gives women the hope to change their lives.

Sons of Thunder, MOST (Men Opposing Sex Trafficking)
Mama Scar is a living testament to the power of love and grace. Her heart overflows with kindness for everyone she encounters, whether through Women of Alabaster or the countless lives she touches as a friend and mentor. She walks in the footsteps of Christ, radiating His words through every act of service. To the broken, she brings healing. To the abandoned, she offers hope. She is not just a voice of faith—she is its hands and feet, shaping futures and transforming lives.

Appreciation

From Scarlet Hudson, Founder of Women of Alabaster

With appreciation for the brave women who have walked the streets, not of gold, but of hell:

To those who have survived and are yet to survive. To those 43 women the Lord determined needed to be home with Him. I thank you all for trusting this dedicated group of volunteers, board members and those of us serving you daily full-time each day. You are courageous and brave to step out of the chaos and take back the life God destined for you.

Psalm 139:10-18
*10 ...even there your hand will guide me, your right hand will hold me fast. 11 If I say, "Surely the darkness will hide me and the light become night around me,"
12 even the darkness will not be dark to you; the night will shine like the day, for darkness is as light to you. 13 For you created my inmost being; you knit me together in my mother's womb. 14 I praise you because I am fearfully and wonderfully made; your works are wonderful, I know that full well. 15 My frame was not hidden from you when I was made in the secret place, when I was woven together in the depths of the earth. 16 Your eyes saw my unformed body; all the days ordained for me were written in your book before one of them came to be.
17 How precious to me are your thoughts, God! How vast is the sum of them! 18 Were I to count them, they would outnumber the grains of sand—when I awake, I am still with you. NIV*

Each of you has tremendous gifts and talents to share with the world. Run, you who are all stronger than the storms you have escaped. Run with the One who has never left you or forgotten you. Each day we pray the Lord would give us just one that we could help leave, and as always, He has been faithful to give us each woman in this book.

Matthew 11:28
There, Jesus says, "Come to me, all you who are weary and burdened, and I will give you rest." This is an open invitation, extended to those who are willing to come. NIV

With appreciation for my husband, Bob:
Thank you for showing me what it means to be loved without fear and loving me "sacrificially." Thank you for inspiring me to say, "Yes," even when it's hard, and for leading me daily. Thank you for your selfless gift of unconditional love, compassion, kindness and understanding. Thank you for showing me Christ in all you say and do and treating me like I am worthy.

Ephesians 5:22-24
22 Wives, submit to your own husbands, as to the Lord. 23 For the husband is head of the wife, as also Christ is head of the church; and He is the Savior of the body. 24 Therefore, just as the church is subject to Christ, so let the wives be to their own husbands in everything. NIV

With appreciation for my sister in the Lord, Nancy:
I know this has been a great challenge with all the stories and personalities, but you, my friend, have the patience of Job. Without you, this would not be possible, and I could never express my gratitude in words.

With appreciation for the present and past WOA Board:
Without each of you, this mission the Lord gave me would not be possible.

With appreciation for the volunteers, donors, and staff:
Thank you for reminding me that walking with brothers and sisters in Christ is the only way to fulfill the Great Commission of Christ.

Matthew 28:16-20
Then the eleven disciples went to Galilee, to the mountain where Jesus had told them to go. When they saw Him, they worshipped Him: but some doubted. Then Jesus came to them and said, "All authority in Heaven and Earth has been given to me. Therefore go and make disciples of all nations, baptizing them in the Name of the Father and the Son and of the Holy Spirit, and teaching them to obey everything I have commanded you, And surely I am with you always, to the very end of the age." NIV

With appreciation for my Lord and Savior:
I pray we have served you well. Thank you for trusting me with your most precious daughters; for not letting me stop when times get hard; for teaching me to breathe in You; and for always being there to listen, lead and direct the path which you have me on. I am your Daughter, and I Love You!

AUTHOR'S APPRECIATION

Thanks to Jesus Christ, our Redeemer and Savior, for through you, life on earth has meaning, and eternal life in heaven is a promise. Thank you for saving me from me.

Thanks to Scarlet Hudson for trusting me to write the story of Women of Alabaster. I am humbled by your confidence in me. Thank you for answering God's call to bring the Gospel of salvation to the oppressed and to sound the alarm of awareness and resources to eradicate homelessness, human trafficking and drug abuse from our society.

Thanks to Darrell Hulshult, my husband and partner in ministry, for your unconditional love and support through the days and nights of my writing and endless verbal processing.

Thanks to Sheryl Burk, my literary consultant, editor, and lifelong friend. Sheryl served in education and ministry in Hamilton, Ohio, before she retired. She continues to serve as an advocate for at-risk children in the children's services system as a Court Appointed Special Advocate.

Thanks to Debbie Day, my literary consultant, editor, and lifelong friend. Debbie was an integral part of inner city ministries when she served in education and ministry with me in Hamilton, Ohio. The "Dream House" began with her vision to help the homeless by providing temporary housing and spiritual support. Debbie is retired and is still serving children in South Carolina with her son and grandchildren.

Thanks to Mary Lou Hudek, my editor, lifelong friend, and Ukeladies partner. We enjoy playing ukuleles and piano duets at Women of Alabaster.

Thanks to the contributors, who took their time to tell their emotional stories connected to Women of Alabaster. May God bless you for your courage and contribution to this collection of God's impact on your lives.

Thanks to the WOA volunteers, "these brave and beautiful people, who willingly serve in dark places, witness what can't be erased, cry knowing they will cry again, and clothe themselves in trauma that wasn't theirs. Today and every day, we are grateful for the warriors who show up to fight for those who can't." - Anita Ridener

Thanks to Denise Chaney of NarratusCreative, for your graphic design and inspiration for people to tell their stories.

PURPOSE OF THIS BOOK

From Scarlet Hudson, Founder of Women of Alabaster

When Scarlet Hudson and I met to discuss the writing of this book, she listed four reasons for people to read about Women of Alabaster:

1. To better understand the heart of the Father for the lost and broken
2. To answer the call to action
3. To ask, "How can I help?"
4. To hear Scar's heart, or as she says, "My yes" and what it has meant for her to follow her heart in serving through Women of Alabaster ministries

Readers will also see in this book:

- the impact that one individual can make on the world

- the contagious nature of one person's story to mobilize another to serve

- a broader scope of acute, chronic, and complex trauma and its consequences that can cycle through generations if gone untreated. In the case of WOA's volunteers, women in recovery, and women still in need of recovery, their transparent stories provide readers insight into the effects of home, school, and work life on decisions made as adolescents and adults.

- the need for your prayers, as well as the power of prayer and Scripture that energizes Scarlet, who energizes her volunteers, who energize needy women as they tap into the transformative process toward shalom (peace and wholeness) through Women of Alabaster

- the power of collaboration and community when local ministries, churches, government agencies, and other organizations combine resources for more effective results

- the responsibility that we have to care, and by caring, giving what we can with what we have for those who are crying out for relief from dire circumstances

All proceeds of this book support Women of Alabaster
To donate or to learn more: www.womenofalabaster.org

To schedule Scarlet Hudson and others for speaking engagements:
scarlet@womenofalabaster.org

To speak to Scarlet:
513-543-5656

To send donation by check written to "Women of Alabaster":
7716 Arlington Rd. Dillsboro, IN 47018

FOREWORD

By Sheryl Burk

Nancy asked me to be her "literary consultant" for this book over lunch at True West. I remember saying something like, "I'll do it, of course, but I need to visit Women of Alabaster with you. I need to see the place, feel the place, so I can help you help others see and feel the ministry."

If you know me, you know that I wear what I'm feeling on my face. In high school, my math teacher would sigh, and ask, "Alright, Johnson (my maiden name), what is it that's confusing you now?"

But the day of my first visit to Women of Alabaster, Nancy could not read my face. I don't think I've ever been so moved and so humbled and so overwhelmed simultaneously. I struggled to process what was happening in those basement rooms of the church on Seventh Street.

I had brought some clothing to donate and spent most of my time in the "shop" where one lady at a time would choose an outfit for the week. One "shopper" shared her morning experience, life in a tent by the river with a married couple, both in addiction, screaming at one another. She continued the story as she sorted through the sweatshirts. When she and the married woman finally left the tent, they heard a gunshot. "The wife went running back, thinking the worst, but the husband was merely playing with her head. He was by the water; the gun under a blanket in the tent."

My school administrator brain went into "safety issue" mode. But the Women of Alabaster volunteer merely said, "Relationships are really hard for people in addiction." She had listened. She acknowledged. She spoke truth over the story.

At the dining table, when I exited the "shop," a woman wept. Bowing her head over the table, shaking it from side to side, she told the story of her recent release from jail. She had only the clothes she was wearing, no ride, no money, no place to go. "I prayed," she tearfully shared, "for someone to drive by where I was walking and offer help." Two ladies did stop, providing her a sack lunch and a blanket. God's angels.

"This is America," I thought to myself, outraged. "Can't we do better than that for a person who has completed jail time?" I was learning a sad societal truth.

I kept thinking, "These women are homeless in my city, suffering, many without adequate care." This truth overwhelmed me. In those basement rooms I saw both pain and beauty. Women of Alabaster provides light for women living in the darkness of homelessness, addiction, and sometimes human trafficking.

Jesus would have taken each woman in His arms, would have offered her healing, peace, and truth. That's what Women of Alabaster is all about. Being Jesus for homeless women in addiction by meeting them just as they are. Providing a place of safety, comfort, and care. Encouraging and supporting the broken. Seeking recovery and renewal for these women through the power and name of Jesus.

I opened my heart and checkbook that day to Women of Alabaster. My prayer is that Nancy's storytelling about the women who find peace in a church basement moves you in a similar way as she paints a picture of these beautiful souls, who are so much more than their circumstances.

INTRODUCTION

Sex Trading in the Bible:
The redemption of Lot's daughters

Readers may be shocked, amazed, and dismayed by the biblical account of Lot and his family living in Sodom. In Genesis 19, two angels entered the city of Sodom planning to spend the night in the city square, but Lot graciously invited them to his home to wash their feet, eat, and sleep in comfort. Before they had gone to bed, every man of every age came from every corner of the city to Lot's house with the intention of having sex with them. In biblical times, showing hospitality to neighbors and strangers was a way to show love and compassion. The concept is turning strangers into friends through love; the Greek word for "hospitality" is "philoxenia" or "loving strangers." In the case of Lot and his angel guests, the entire city of men wanted to physically, sexually "love" or rape these strangers.

They called to Lot, "Where are the men who came to you tonight? Bring them out to us so that we can have sex with them." - Genesis 19:5

This shocking request shows the level of perversion of Sodom that suggests multiple acts that may or may not have been consensual, but definitely wicked, as Lot described it. He tried to protect his guests by offering his two virgin daughters to the crowd instead, specifying that the men could do anything they wanted with them.

> Lot went outside to meet them and shut the door behind him 7 and said, "No, my friends. Don't do this wicked thing. 8 Look, I have two daughters who have never slept with a man. Let me bring them out to you, and you can do what you like with them. But don't do anything to these men, for they have come under the protection of my roof." - Genesis 19:6-8 NIV

In the culture of the times and in the depraved city of Sodom, Lot felt that his role as host superseded his role as father. He thought it better to sacrifice his own daughters (his property) than to offer the lives of the angels (his male guests) to the wicked crowd.

God intervened as the angels pulled Lot back inside, shut the door, and blinded the crowd of men so that they could not find the door. The angels told Lot to gather his family, and they led them out of Sodom before the city was completely destroyed.

Not only the daughters, but Lot's family, were redeemed from destruction of

Sodom and Gomorrah. The only exception was Lot's wife, who disobeyed and looked back, turning into a pillar of salt. However, the story doesn't tell how the daughters felt at the moment when they were facing rape and sodomy from a crowd of men, who were given permission to do so by their father. Women were the lowest level of society and treated like property.

Today, women may agree (or not) that we have risen above the cultural chains and oppression of society, but many of our sisters are being treated as property through sex trafficking, prostitution, domestic violence, and street violence associated with homelessness. (Men and boys are also involved in these sins of our society.) These evils are not new to modern times. The trauma and violence associated with prostitution and sex trafficking impact the individuals directly involved, their families, and all of us as a society.

The two angels in Lot's home stopped the intended abuse of his two daughters. Today, there is an angel who ministers to women on the streets and provides a safe haven to help stop their oppressive lifestyle. She calls her ministry "Women of Alabaster," offering food, clothing, showers, prayer, devotions, and a way to escape their oppressors through community facilities, programs, and resources. That angel, Scarlet Hudson, is called "The General" by her volunteers because she leads the war against sin and violence toward women. On the streets, women call her "Mama Scar" or simply "Scar." Her goal is to show them the love of Jesus and to bring them into salvation and a loving relationship with him.

Prayer Journal of Mama Scar:

12/4/2004 - Promise from God

"For I know the plans I have for you," says the Lord. "They are plans for your good and not for disaster to give you a future and a hope. 12 In those days when you pray, I will listen." 13 If you look for me in earnest, you will find me when you seek me. 14 I will be found by you," says the Lord. "I will end your captivity and restore your fortunes. I will gather you out of the nations where I sent you and bring you home again to your own land."
- Jeremiah 29:11-14 NLT

Chapter 1

Women of Alabaster's Day Center Hamilton, Ohio

$\mathcal{F}$rom a church parking lot through an alley in the inner city of Hamilton, Ohio, I lock my car doors and walk to the back of an historical brick and stone church to the back double doors, unlocked and unmarked, except for a small bumper sticker sized sign that says, "Women of Alabaster." One of the doors stands slightly opened for me to peek inside to the top of a set of stairs leading down into the bowels of the church. I pull the door open and step around a large well-used backpack stuffed to the breaking zippers. I side step past a small makeshift grocery cart to grab onto the railing. I make my way down the worn carpeted steps toward the dim light at the bottom of the stairs. I listen for signs of life beyond the light to hear sounds of laughter and women chatting.

Rounding the stairwell, I walk into a large well lighted room carpeted and decorated with a sofa, some chairs, some holiday decorations, and a couple of vanities with makeup and toiletries. Verses of Scripture were stenciled on the walls with various framed motivational pictures. The chatter is coming from the kitchen at the end of the room, and I can see some women's faces smiling and eating from paper bowls.

Since they were engaged in conversation, I took time to peek into the side room full of women's used clothing and slightly worn shoes, all neatly organized on racks. The next door opening led to a shower room. Across from there was a dimly lit room with the door cracked open. I could see blue camping cots lined along the wall.

The room beside it opened to a devotional space with comfy couches, a TV, Bibles, and artificial flowers. It reminded me of a church youth room minus the games and snacks.

In the middle of the great room was a small wooden dinette with three chairs that looked like they came right out of a home of the 1980's. In the center of the table were stacks of art paper and paint brushes. One woman was intently painting a nondescript image of bright yellow hues while she talked quietly to herself without pausing to notice if anyone was listening to her, or answering her. She had the aging signs of a 70-year-old woman in a 35-year-old body, possibly because she lacked routine hair appointments, day spas, and Oil of Olay Regenerist moisturizer. Her shoulders were rounded, head bent forward, wrinkled patchy skin, some bruises on her arms and legs, and an ashen face that hid her eyes from me. Her ratty hair band was not doing its job, and if her clothes matched at any point in time, the extra layers discounted any recognizable style.

You know the woman that I describe. You have seen her walking alone on the streets of your home town or resting against the lightpost of the local White Castle curled with her knees tucked inside her sweatshirt to keep warm. You have seen her stumbling ahead of a borrowed shopping cart or nudged along by her pimp. If you saw her, you probably kept driving because of the surrounding neighborhood, or you didn't want to be accused of soliciting on the streets. Maybe you said a prayer or made a donation to the cause, or maybe you complained to yourself about the conditions of society today. But for me, today, she just became real, and her life situation became personal to me and to the volunteers at the Women of Alabaster Day Center.

At the doorway of the kitchen, I caught the attention of the leader of this place. After a warm welcome and a hug, Scarlet led me to her office to tell me more about the people and the projects that fill her heart to the brim.

For two days per week for three hours, women are welcomed to come and rest, shower, eat, refresh their clothes, pray, and receive spiritual and mental health support from several compassionate women who volunteer to meet their basic needs for the moment. The volunteers stand ready to connect them to a rehab center, a homeless shelter, a hospital, an emergency room, or wherever they can get help for them.

Prayer Journal of Mama Scar:
11/2015 - Promise from God

6 Don't worry about anything; instead, pray about everything. Tell God what you need, and thank him for all he has done. 7 If you do this, you will experience God's peace, which is far more wonderful than the human mind can understand. His peace will guard your hearts and minds as you live in Christ Jesus. - Philippians 4:6-7 NLT

Who are the Women of Alabaster? Who are the women who volunteer here? Who are the women who come here for help? Who started this ministry? And what is the significance of the alabaster jar in their name, their logo that is a tilted, broken jar, and the message on the volunteers' shirts that say, "Leave her alone!"?

Let's begin with stories and testimonies from the women themselves.

Chapter 2

"For a long time, I never knew what my calling was."
— Leah

*T*he Day Centers in Hamilton and Cincinnati are warm and welcoming places for the worn and the weary. From word of mouth, posted signs in the jails, or invitations from the jail ministries, women find their way to the door that leads them away from violence and loneliness to a temporary refuge of safety. They enjoy a clean and quiet place to rest, a hot shower, a clean set of clothing, and a hot meal. All the elements of biblical Hebrew hospitality are present, where strangers from the outside are treated like family on the inside. In addition to the tasteful setting and tasty food, the women find a friend in the servant hostess, who greets them with kindness, sits and talks with them at the table, listens to their hearts, and prays blessings over them before they return to the street. In Hamilton, this servant hostess is Leah.

Along with her inner beauty, Leah has the outward beauty that one would expect from her career as a hair stylist for 22 years. Her long, wavy blonde hair, huge hooped earrings, and athletic form accentuate her sparkling green eyes and beaming smile that exudes warmth to every visitor to the center. Her strength and beauty are fueled by intercessory prayer on Monday nights at the Hamilton Dream Center, an inner city church located just a few yards from the doors of the Day Center where Leah first met Scarlet Hudson. Scarlet's ministry was familiar to Leah, but Leah did not see how she could contribute, other than through prayer. However, God had been pulling her in the direction of Women of Alabaster years before. Leah said, "For a long time, I never knew what my calling was."

According to Leah, "I had my hands anointed about 15 years ago, because I thought that there were women coming to me that I would never get to pray for outwardly, but my hands would be outwardly touching them as I styled their hair." A client from the hair salon had given Leah a sign to put above her work station that said, "Her Chair Her Ministry," but she still didn't recognize it as having a special calling.

Leah says that she has always loved the Lord and has never known a time when she has not loved him. She didn't have a testimony of deep darkness and sin that led to a dramatic salvation story, but she did go through a time of testing and heartache. Within a three year period, Leah lost her mother, her father, and her father-in-law. She also experienced a painful onslaught of rheumatoid arthritis, and she felt the Lord telling her to slow down at work.

"I told my husband that God put me in a place where I don't know what he has for me, but there's something coming, and I need to slow down working. He said that he was 100% behind me and that I should do what God says."

A couple of days later in Sunday service, Leah's pastor was preaching and looked down at her and said, "You know what God has told you to do. I don't know if it's to slow down, so listen. I'm not sure it is, but you need to listen to what he said."

Leah looked at my husband, who said to her, "Wow! Was he in our kitchen when we were talking?"

Leah continued into a season of talking to the Lord about her calling. Her clients at the hair salon had asked her to lead a Bible study, so she said yes. Twenty-five women came to the study. She started volunteering more at her church. When one of the women mentioned taking Thanksgiving leftovers to Women of Alabaster, Leah went with her, telling her friend that God had been dealing with her heart about volunteering there. Again, she said yes.

Not long after, Leah became the Hamilton Day Center Coordinator every Tuesday and Thursday, when they are open. On alternate days, Leah continued her ministry in her hair styling chair. Nervous about what she could offer to Women of Alabaster, Leah heard God speaking to her, saying, "You have loved women well from behind your hair styling chair for 22 years. That's the same thing these women need, just someone to love them."

Leah says, "I make sure everything is running smoothly. I get to the Day Center early and open up, get the coffee started and the drinks made. I coordinate meals, making sure people are bringing food. I clean up after everybody. I like it because it lets me float to the different rooms, so I get to show love to the girls and get to hear their stories. I didn't know what to expect coming here. It's intimidating, yet fulfilling. They are everyday girls. Most of them have had major trauma. I began to understand why they are doing what they're doing. I realize that I was a little judgmental before. It has changed my whole perspective about them.

"The first night we went out for street ministry, I met a young girl. She was probably 21, on the street since she was 14. Her mom used drugs and prostituted and had her on the street with her. The mom died when the girl was 14 or 15, so she's been taking care of herself this whole time. She's a beautiful girl. She's the first one I ever met on the street. It broke my heart.

"We traveled around the city, and when we came back, she was sitting by a lamp post over here by White Castle, high. At that point, she was bent over. I looked at Laura, and I said, 'You know what? If this was my life, if I had no hope, I would get high, too.' You understand it after you hear her story. I am sure she is probably violated quite a bit. She's a beautiful little girl, you know?

"I have a 24 year old girl. I couldn't imagine her being on the street. Hearing stories, you find out more of why Women of Alabaster is so needed. These homeless women just need to be loved by somebody. It's that simple."

Two teams go out for street ministry in the evenings. They take hygiene bags that contain toothbrushes and toothpaste, bars of soap, washcloths, socks, chapsticks, deodorant, snacks, and small bottles of water. If it's cold outside, they give mittens and hats and little hand warmers, along with bags of peanut butter and jelly, chips, and water bottles. The teams know where most of the women hang out, so they go to them to see what they need. The teams pray with the women and hope to find at least one new girl each time. Says Leah, "We want to let them know we're here. Generally, they always come. I have not ever had any girl refuse prayer."

More often than not, the women are aware of some sense of God with a range of beliefs, but their childhood traumas or life experiences leave them stuck in present day conflicts. One woman told Leah, "You know, I believe in the Lord and I have faith in him, but I love my sin too much right now."

Leah responded, "That's the realest thing anybody's ever told me. You're not wrong for that, for being honest, but there is a sanctification process. You don't have to clean yourself up to go to the Lord. You go to him, and then he is going to help you give up those things."

The woman said, "I know. I'm just not ready yet." After praying together, the woman left the Day Center, and Leah will be praying for her and will be ready to lead her to a safer place for restoration and rehabilitation.

Leah prays, "God, don't let me come in here and get jaded. Help me to love them, even through things that I don't quite understand."

One woman came to the Day Center with an issue of domestic violence. After checking for available shelters and finding no availability, she called her son. He said that he had talked to his wife and that she could come and stay with them for awhile, but short term. He said that she couldn't stay with them forever. The woman told Leah, "I don't want to go there and mess things up. I know I'm difficult." She said that his daughter had just tried to kill herself at 16, and then she said, "My son tried to kill himself when he was 18."

Leah asked the woman, "So this is a generational depression?" She said yes, that she was raped when her son was little and was in the same room sleeping. The man had told her that if she made any noise or anything, that he would kill the baby. That was a very heavy day for Leah, who went home and thought, "What did I sign up for? This is a lot!"

"This is a cross, and we have got to be prayed up. We can take this stuff home with us and it can affect our life, too. Scarlet has been teaching me that there are going to be times when you are trying to help a woman, and she is going to say that she doesn't want the help. That's what happened. The same woman came back on the same day, and she is back on the street. After crying with her and worrying about her all week, I learned that I can do what I can do, and the rest is up to the women, and hopefully, God can get ahold of them."

Leah recalls a success story after she had only volunteered for six months: "I was fixing a woman a plate of food, and I looked back at her just sweating. She looked at me and said, 'I've got to get out of this life or I'm going to die.' I thought she was hot from the walk here, but she was withdrawing.

"I asked her, 'What are we going to do about it? Let's get you in somewhere, to a rehab right now.' She had been doing an 8-ball of fentanyl a day, which is $260 a day. I said, 'I can't afford $260 a day in drugs. How can you?'

"She said, 'By doing things that I said I would never do.' She had injected herself in her neck and had bruises all down her neck. I had never seen that in my life. We brought her in here and cleaned out her bags. Thank God Scarlet was here that day. There were used needles, which we got rid of. Obviously, she couldn't take that with her to rehab. She was just crying and crying. We got her some clothes packed up and called a place, and they were going to take her.

"Scarlet asked me, 'Do you know if she's accepted the Lord or not?'

"I didn't know. So I asked her, 'Have you ever asked Jesus into your life?'

"She said, 'I will after I get cleaned up. I know that's the demons telling me that.'

"I said, 'It is. You get saved right now and give your heart to God, and you let him do the rest.' She said she wanted to, so we prayed with her. We actually baptized her while she was here. She sat on a little chair, and we got buckets and we baptized her. It was beautiful. She cried and cried and cried. She called her mom and told her that she was going to rehab. And this was my first time dealing with this.

"The mom was not happy to talk to her. It was breaking my heart, but I realize that her mom has probably been through hell with her. Scarlet and I put her in a car, and Scar took her to rehab, and she is probably, at this point, almost 200 days clean. I see her walking out, and she comes to group at church. She has gone through long term recovery. She is working. She has meat on her bones, because she was so thin from using drugs. Her eyes are so bright. So that was my first success story. This is pretty cool. This works.

"And if we see 50 women, and only 1 gets help, then we've done it. It was worth it, and that's what keeps us going."

When Leah goes home from volunteering at the Day Center, she listens to worship music on the way home, takes a nap for about 20 minutes, and asks God to bless each girl that comes to the Day Center.

Leah continues taking trauma training sessions with Scarlet and has an eye on the future of ministry with Women of Alabaster: "I'm excited to see what else we're getting ready to do. Maybe this would become my full time job, ministry. My son graduates this year; that financial burden is going to be gone, so I can quit my job and do this. My children know me, and they know that I'm going to do what God wants of me. I hope my stories minister to them, too." Leah has found her calling.

Prayer Journal of Mama Scar:

2/15/2022 - Promise from God

We declare Numbers 33:53 that we shall dispossess the inhabitants of the land and dwell in it, for I have given you the land to possess. Lord, Your Word says in Deuteronomy 1:8 See, I have set land before you, go in and possess the land which the Lord swore unto your fathers, Abraham, Isaac, and Jacob, to give unto them and to their seed after them. NKJV

And Lord, Your Word in Joshua 1:15-17 says to take possession of the land the Lord Your God is going to give them. Then they will have a place to rest like you do. After that, you may go back and take possession of the land east of the Jordan River, which the Lord's servant Moses gave you. Lord, I declare this 46 acres of land for the girls' portion of the earth for their complete healing. This land will be a living testimony to their salvation stories to the goodness of their God.

I BELIEVE, LORD! I BELIEVE IN YOU AND YOUR PROMISES ARE YES AND AMEN. TO YOUR GLORY, LORD! AMEN AND AMEN!

Chapter 3

"Miss Fashionista"
— Gina

Most people are familiar with the adage, "Clothes make the man," meaning that dressing well influences how people perceive us. At Women of Alabaster, the "clothes make the woman," not for the purposes of influencing how others perceive them, but for influencing how they perceive themselves. Feeling depressed, neglected, and perhaps abused in the streets, the women come to the Day Center to feel renewed and revived again. A hot shower and new outfit can make any woman feel better, but access to a nice shower room and clothing closet is a huge draw for those visiting Women of Alabaster two days a week.

Donations of clothing and shoes come from all over the community, and they are organized into a makeshift clothing closet for visitors to choose a free outfit per week and a free pair of shoes per month. A mannequin displays the "outfit of the week" or "outfit of the day" as a guide for coordinating separates and accessories. Next to the freestore styled closet is another room of career type clothing reserved for women going to job interviews.

The woman with the skills and passion for fashion to maintain the clothing closets is Gina, the one they call "Miss Fashionista.. Gina's own personal look is stylish, attractive, and welcoming. Her black and silver cropped and spiked hairstyle highlights her rich brown eyes and bright white smile. With a peachy skin tone and dangling earrings, Gina's whole demeanor says "fashion!" Her delightful love of people and clothing makes me want to shop in the clothes closet myself.

The women call her "Miss Fashionista" because of her eye for seasonal, practical, trendy clothes. She organizes and designs the makeshift clothing closet to mimic a department store as she assists every "shopper" in making smart choices. The women are allotted 5-10 minutes each to pick out clothes. They enter the mini-store looking depressed and dressed in well-worn garbs that make them visual targets in the street. However, after a few minutes with Gina, they emerge from the clothing closet transformed into modest outfits and glowing faces. If time permits, Gina or Leah or other volunteers will treat the women to a makeover with new hair styles and makeup. All of this outward transformation helps to lead the women toward seeking transformation inwardly, both physically and spiritually.

On any given day, the Day Center has served as many as 20 women ranging in age from 18 to mid-60's. Gina serves in any capacity as needed. She helps with shower duty and ensures that each woman gets 15 minutes to shower. She serves food, prays with and listens to them, but where the women most like her to be is in the clothing closet. Gina takes from her experience as a volunteer with her friend at a boutique. She knows that every woman wants to look pretty, even those who are homeless or addicts. She "glams them up," as she says.

Gina says of her volunteer work, "You can see a countenance change from the moment they walk in until the moment they leave. We try to feed them the Word, pray for them, and let them know that this is a safe place where they can share anything they need to share. Prayer makes a difference on how a day goes."

Gina met Scarlet years ago at Church On Fire under Pastor Doug Combs. She was intrigued with what Scarlet did, and it was something that stuck with her. Although Gina was working full time, she would put together baskets for the women at Christmas time. Included in the baskets were leggings wrapped up with body care products, along with a note that said, "Jesus loves you, and so do I."

Although Gina wished to do more for Women of Alabaster, she was involved in caring for her family. For a time, Gina helped to take care of her grandsons and her mother, who passed away last year. Meanwhile, she kept praying about volunteering with Scarlet. One day she toured the facility with Scarlet and met some of the girls. Instantly, she knew that she needed to be in this ministry. She talked with her husband and made a decision completely on faith to step away from her job as a loan officer at a credit union. Previously, she was a scrub tech in Labor and Delivery, so her medical background has also helped her to help the girls with simple wound care.

Says Gina about her "yes" to God: "I felt peace about doing that, and I had not felt peace about leaving before. It was a huge leap of faith because it meant no income. I said that I was going to live off my savings and let God provide, and he has so far. It has been almost a year. Instantly, I made a connection with every girl here. The workers and I are friends. We're very close, like sisters. The women that we serve here are like an extension of my friends, so I look forward to seeing them every week. Not that I want to see them here; I would rather that they were in their own apartment and doing well with rehab, not on the streets or living in tents or cars anymore."

Gina sees her purpose in showing the love of Jesus to every woman that comes into the Day Center. "I love that when they come in, they see a warm smile; they get a huge hug every time. They are told that we love them, and hopefully, they know it and feel that. It makes a difference. They have told us that Women of Alabaster is unlike anything that they have ever felt in any church or any service. I tell them that what they are getting here is an extension of our own faith, our own relationship with Christ. I say that we are pouring out what we have and pouring into them. That's the difference for us.

"Imagine being on the street and you're scared that someone is going to attack you or steal your things, which happens. They stay up a lot during the night and try to sleep during the day, so we offer them a sleeping room where they can get a couple hours of uninterrupted sleep.

"Hygiene is important. The women need showers because many of them have wounds, skin conditions, or infections from drug use. We have bandages, Tylenol, Neosporin, and other minimal over the counter aides to help minor medical needs.

"The women need a change of clothes because most of them are carrying their life in their backpacks and bags – literally. They have no way to wash their clothes. They can't afford to go to a laundromat. We don't have any way to wash them here, so 75% of the time, they throw their old outfits away because they are dirt encrusted or extremely soiled. A shower and clean set of clothes help them to feel normal and not like a castoff of society.

"When they leave here, they have such smiles on their faces, even though they're going right back into what they just came out of. They're leaving with a little more pep in their step, a little more joy, and it's because of what we do here. I hope to continue volunteering for Women of Alabaster until Jesus comes back."

Gina also goes to the jail with Scarlet for a recovery group on Thursday evening. When she first started, she shared, "I bawled my head off all the time because it was something that I had never done. Now I love going to the jail. I love seeing the girls and getting the hugs. If they want to get baptized, we baptize them with a cup of water over a trash can. We have some of the best conversations in the strangest of places. We're helping to guide them when they leave, where they're supposed to go, and what their paths will be."

A favorite success story for Gina is the Be Strong girls, who live two doors down from the Hamilton Day Center. They live in a house in a two-year recovery program. Gina has gotten to know them in the neighborhood and at a conference. One of the girls is almost finished with her program, and she said, "I want to do what you do. I want to help other girls out of what I came out of." Gina knows their life experiences will be of value if they serve at Women of Alabaster. She says that they have more knowledge of what a person is going through because they just came out of it.

In Celebrate Recovery and in the jail, Gina says to the girls, "I don't look at what you do or what you did. I look at you. I see you. You don't even see you. You don't see what God has planned for you. It is amazing. You have a life outside of this jail cell. He has a plan for you, and it is good.

"To get help, all the girls have to do is to say, 'Yes, I need help. Today is the day.' We're going to call everyone that we have connections with. Scarlet has an entire list. She will call and try to get them into a home immediately, a group home, an apartment, somewhere to get out of their abusive situation.

"We have one girl that comes in and tells everyone how many days she has been clean, but she's still living on the street with her husband. They have a place, but I don't know where it is or if it is safe. If you don't get to the root of the cause of the addiction, they're never going to be free. Most of the girls have had abuse in their past or a missing family unit or they had older siblings that started issues with them, or a father or step-brother.

"The best compliment I have ever received came from a girl here who said, 'My friend wanted me to let you know that when she came here, she felt the peace of God with you. You really have God all over you, and you can see it. And you can feel it.'

"I said, 'Thank you so much.' You always wonder if you're doing the right thing, and if you're doing it enough. I don't need to be puffed up. I don't need a pedestal. I'd be happy to serve by just giving them a shower bag and a towel. I don't need notoriety. I just need to be here for them. I need God's presence because I can't do this in Gina. I have to do it with God.

Prayer Journal of Mama Scar:

2/16/2022 - The Waiting

To fulfill sometimes takes time. Wait for it. Be patient. Daniel 9:2 says,

"'In the first year of his reign, I, Daniel, perceived in the books the number of years that, according to the word of the Lord to Jeremiah the prophet, must pass before the end of the desolations of Jerusalem, namely, seventy years.'"

The years in waiting for Messiah's return can be challenging. We know who we are waiting for and what He brings in His coming again. Complete peace and love will cover the New Jerusalem. There will be no striving, no fighting, just living with and worshiping our Lord. Oh, what a wonderful time that will be.

We are given so much hope from the scriptures. It gives us the courage to follow the Lord and while waiting, worship Him from our place here until His coming. We must learn to experience Heaven on Earth now so we catch a glimpse of His Glory and Power. We love You, Lord, and are waiting for Your return.

Chapter 4

"Now I look at the stained glass differently." — Stephanie

Stephanie grew up in a religious family that went to a church with stained glass windows. They would talk about the rites and duties of belonging, but she doesn't remember talking about a relationship with Jesus. Stephanie was a rebellious teenager who continued her rebellion in college, where she met her husband. They were married in a cathedral-like church in Springfield, Ohio, filled more with ornamentation than God's Holy Spirit. They made attempts at attending church on a weekly basis, but after the second time of her husband sleeping in the very last pew through the entire service, they stopped attending.

Stephanie worked in physical therapy at a clinic, and one of her clients invited her to a non-denominational mega church. Stephanie and her husband accepted the invitation to try church again. They were new to the concept of raised hands during worship, people carrying their own Bibles, and such a huge community of believers. Stephanie joined a ministry called Alpha, a 14-week process of having some of her questions answered, where even more questions surfaced about giving her life to Christ.

One night on the way home, she was angry, saying to her husband, "I don't understand what these people have in our little group." She began crying and threw her Bible on the floor of the car.

She asked her husband, "Why does everybody have this, and I don't? What's wrong with me?"

At that moment, right then and there, she says that she was slain by the Holy

Spirit, like a bolt of lightning. Her husband said, "I don't know what happened, but you were just saved." That night her life changed forever. A month later, her husband was saved. When Stephanie and her husband changed churches to be closer to home, Stephanie started a running program, called "Mothers Making Strides," which supported a backpack program to feed school children over the weekends. The program grew and became successful for 10 years until COVID shut it down.

A personal crisis shut all of her ministering down. For two years, the Lord worked on Stephanie toward healing her marriage. However, as she shared, "I still had this rejection spirit on me since childhood. My dad transferred all the time with his company, so I was always making friends and losing friends." When Stephanie had become a Christian, she hadn't expected that she would have friends leave her.

Even though the Lord poured into Stephanie for those two years, she felt so broken that she couldn't pour into anyone else. Then she met Leah, who was friends with one of Stephanie's good friends. "I started with, 'Oh, my gosh, I love your hair! I'm going to come to YOU to do my hair!' Last October, as I was sitting in her chair at the hair salon, Leah said, 'This lady came to my church and spoke about this ministry called Women of Alabaster.' I said, 'Oh, my gosh, can I have her number?'"

For a second time, Stephanie's life changed. She went to an open house for Women of Alabaster and met Scarlet Hudson, who has since become her mentor. Scarlet's motherly ways of guiding Stephanie were important because of losing her own mother six years ago from Alzheimer's.

Stephanie says that the Lord was telling her that she was ready to serve people again. She says, "Always, but especially now, my heart is to serve people. I had lived in Chicago for a long time with homeless people in my neighborhood. I would always pay for the weekly 'streetwise paper' that they sold through a program by Depaul University that printed newspapers for them to sell. This news is about everything happening on the streets, good and bad, that is not in the Chicago Tribune, the big paper. The homeless people have 'blocks' or 'territories' where they would sell the street news regularly, and I would buy a paper every week. There was lots of prostitution, transgender prostitution, in my neighborhood, even though it was considered a safe neighborhood. It was a whole new experience for me."

Stephanie's first experience at Women of Alabaster involved a girl that she had helped to take to drug rehab. When the girl had a relapse, Stephanie felt destroyed. Then she thought, "Wait. This is not about me. I'm just the vessel. I just want to be the vessel for God to use me. Now the woman has been clean for three years and is doing well.

A most memorable girl came into the Day Center asking for help. "I need help, and I need Jesus." She was baptized right away and taken immediately into one of the rehab centers.

The next week, Scarlet called Stephanie and said, "They're kicking her out. There is another place that has a bed. Can you take her?" Stephanie postponed her appointments immediately and took her to a center for rehabilitation for methamphetamine. There Stephanie learned about the red tape associated with the two-hour admittance process. They didn't accept her CareSource insurance, which she had shown them upon her arrival. Rejected again, the girl texted her "dope boy" to come and pick her up. Stephanie asked her to hold off until she could see if any other places would admit her. After multiple calls, a center in Dayton agreed to send a car to pick her up and admit her to their facility. Stephanie took her to get food while they waited.

Once the woman had gotten through the program, her parents let her come home, although they had endured 20 years of lies, stealing, and actions that wreck relationships. Stephanie has since lost contact with her and her family. She continues to pray for their healing and mental health.

Stephanie says, "This is a process. We can't force them. We can't convince them. They know why we're here. They know that we are here to clothe them and feed them and love on them, but we're here also because we have the resources to get them out of that life. It has to be their choice. We can't coerce them. It's between them and God, and what I do is between me and God.

"If I hadn't been broken, if I wasn't actually able to see the Lord picking up the pieces and putting me back together, then I would not be able to tell these women, 'This is what the Lord did for me.' I think a lot of people don't hear you if you merely recite Scripture, especially to people who have never opened a Bible. I find that the connection is sharing what God has done for me, and telling people that He can do it for them, too.

"Now that I am on the other side, I can give thanks to Jesus for the suffering. That's hard to say, but thank you, Jesus."

Stephanie has a different perspective of the outward appearances of church and the inward transformation of souls in a saving relationship with Jesus Christ. "Now I look at glass stained windows differently." The beauty of the glass stained windows is her metaphor for the beauty and the light of Jesus that she feels within herself.

Through my eyes, Stephanie serves as a living "glass stained window" of beauty and light to the women who come out of their darkness to the Day Center. She follows in Mama Scar's footsteps as she shows empathy and love toward the women. About her plans for her future, Stephanie says with enthusiasm, "Scarlet has taught me a lot. I want to be here forever, if she'll let me, and if God allows it."

Prophetic Journal of Mama Scar:

11/9/2015

Arise, Jerusalem! Let your light shine for all the nations to see! For the glory of the Lord is shining upon you. - Isaiah 61:1

I decree and declare that I will be a light for all to see for the Lord God Almighty. He is the light inside of me without which I would live in darkness. I will wait patiently for the fulfillment of all God has for me to do on the earth. I know He is working all things out in the spiritual realm for me to accomplish in the earthly realm. I will not be discouraged by what my eyes can see but by what my spirit man is telling me.

Isaiah 61:1-9 Proclaim Freedom

'The Spirit of the Sovereign Lord is upon me, for the Lord has anointed me to bring good news to the poor. He has sent me to comfort the brokenhearted and to proclaim that captives will be released and prisoners will be freed. He has sent me to tell those who mourn that the time of the Lord 's favor has come, and with it, the day of God's anger against their enemies. To all who mourn in Israel, he will give a crown of beauty for ashes, a joyous blessing instead of mourning, festive praise instead of despair. In their righteousness, they will be like great oaks that the Lord has planted for his own glory. They will rebuild the ancient ruins, repairing cities destroyed long ago. They will revive them, though they have been deserted for many generations. Foreigners will be your servants. They will feed your flocks and plow your fields and tend your vineyards. You will be called priests of the Lord , ministers of our God. You will feed on the treasures of the nations and boast in their riches. Instead of shame and dishonor, you will enjoy a double share of honor. You will possess a double portion of prosperity in your land, and everlasting joy will be yours. "For I, the Lord , love justice. I hate robbery and wrongdoing. I will faithfully reward my people for their suffering and make an everlasting covenant with them. Their descendants will be

recognized and honored among the nations. Everyone will realize that they are a people the Lord has blessed.'" NLT

I decree and declare these 9 verses are being lived in my life. That I was made by God for such a time as this. That the day is today NO MORE fighting what I have been called to do. You, oh God, are upon me and I will see my sisters and brothers set free by the Power and Authority of Jesus Christ! NO ONE we meet should be left behind but come into your Kingdom, Lord, after hearing the gospel of Jesus Christ!

Father, I release all angels you have hovering on my life to come and walk this life out. I release You, Father, to come to me in my spirit and hover NO more. Be active in my life, activate all spiritual wisdom, knowledge, discernment. Power and Authority in my life now today. Do what you must, Lord. Release the ancient Keys, Lord. Release! Release! Release!

I bind the enemy from my life and my husband's life, and I nullify all assignments and cancel any demonic attack in our lives and release the Power and Authority of Jesus Christ in our lives. Amen.

Chapter 5

Women of Alabaster Day Center, Cincinnati, Ohio

After a few weekly visits to the Hamilton Day Center, I was compelled to visit the Cincinnati Day Center to learn more about the ministry and the women there. Scarlet directed me to the address on Central Ave., which is next to City Link and one street away from an area known as "The Block" where prostitution and related crimes are common. Scarlet told me to find the doorbell next to a white double garage door, and someone would buzz me in. Although I had assured my husband that I would be fine going alone, I had moments of hesitation that prompted me to say a quick prayer that came out, "Holy, holy Jesus, where are we going now?"

Going up a couple flights of cement stairs and past a few doors that opened to storage or vacant areas under construction of some sort, I made my way to a door that opened to Scarlet and a few other women. As with the Hamilton Day Center, once I got inside, the atmosphere changed completely to a lighted, warm, decorated, peaceful place. The room for rest had four hospital chairs that opened to make cushioned daybeds. A sitting area had cushioned chairs and a coffee table, and another room was Scarlet's office with seats to host several visitors. On her desk was a bowl of tiny Jesus figures and small prayer cloths with Scripture written on them. When a woman came in to tell her goodbye, Scarlet offered her "a little Jesus" and a prayer cloth. As she shook her hand, Scarlet held onto her hand a little longer and asked if she wanted prayer. The woman smiled and said, "Yes, I would like that very much." The two prayed with hands joined as I sat and bowed my head. I imagined that this was a scene repeated many times in the course of Scarlet's day at the center.

Several women sat around the kitchen table while the director, named Jackie, served delicious smelling food from large aluminum trays: chicken fried rice, green beans in a cream sauce, and more. She offered to microwave any plates that were not hot enough for each person. Scarlet said that the food comes through a group called "Le Soup" that receives excess food from high end restaurants. Each meal has been prepared by a chef, and there seemed to be enough food to feed twenty people or more.

As the women ate, Scarlet attended to one woman whose foot and ankle were quite swollen and soaking in a large bucket. Scarlet filled a pitcher with warm water and poured it over the woman's foot while she enjoyed her food. I was taken aback by the similarities with this scene and the biblical accounts of footwashing: Jesus washing the feet of his disciples, and the woman with the alabaster jar pouring perfume over Jesus' feet. On this day, in an almost vacant facility in the middle of a deserted section of the hood at noon, here was the leader of the Women of Alabaster providing front line care to one of the women from The Block with gentleness and humility. I didn't hear the woman say anything, not even a sigh of relief. She kept her head down and continued quietly eating her meal. I wondered if there were no words to express what she was feeling, either deep pain, temporary relief, hunger being satisfied, or simply peace with no worries for her safety while she was there.

In the next room, a volunteer was busy assisting a woman with a new outfit from the closet of used clothing. Across the narrow hallway was Scarlet's office. She had a couple of women with her. Before I could complete the tour of the Day Center, I learned that I needed to interview a woman who needed to be at her place of work within the hour. This time I was struck by the juxtaposition of past sex workers coming to the center for food, clothing, and safety with the first person I was to interview: a woman who has been sober for six years and who now works for the Addiction Services Council through the Hamilton County Justice Center helping women to leave their street life for healthier lifestyles. I could hardly wait to hear how women end up on the street in sex trafficking but find their way back to safety and security.

Prophetic Journal of Mama Scar:

2/18/2022

America has lost her identity with Me, Your Creator. Freedom is not free. You have put yourself in bondage. You have turned away from the ONE who created you. You curse my name, laugh at My Word. You take My love and step on it. Your conscience, there is none. NO MORALS, ETHICS, just the distorted ones you have created. You have taken My perfect creation and said what I made and How I made man and woman is wrong. Repent and turn around. I, the Lord, am standing right behind. You will have to do the turning. My Son was not enough for you, His life and sacrifice you mock. The sins you are committing He paid for with His very life. My remnant must stand firm. NO COMPROMISE with anyone or anything that goes against My Word. My remnant is getting stronger. The TRUE BRIDE is purifying herself, making herself ready for my return. Tell the people how much I LOVE them and the pain I feel for those lost and away from me. Tell them they must come back. Falling away is not an option for them. There are consequences to their sin. Truth of ME must be told. Find them. Tell them the Gospel. I NEED YOU to do it now. Time is slowing down. Creation is groaning and wars are coming.

Tell them I, ABBA, am waiting.

My Son Yeshua is here and HE has everything you need. Healing Deliverance Freedom is yours. HE IS IN THE ROOM....MOVE TOWARDS MY SON

Chapter 6

"I walked in darkness for a long time." — Jackie

For 21+ years Jackie worked as a hairdresser, and for the past nine years, she has been a private caregiver to the elderly. Every client and patient of Jackie has benefited from her big heart, because she loves ALL people. In 2018 God sent Jackie to Women of Alabaster. Jackie said she knew God wanted her to serve our hurting and victimized friends on the streets. She said she was to "pray for them, walk along side them, encourage them, and let them know God's heart for them." Jackie has done that and more. There is nothing she won't do to love our friends and support the mission of Women of Alabaster.

Jackie leans on Scripture with Jeremiah 29:11 as her favorite:
For I know the plans I have for you, declares the Lord, plans to prosper you and not to harm you, plans to give you hope and a future.

Jackie and I took the stairs down to a level of the Day Center that had a makeshift clinic and other storage areas. The room was small, and our chairs were close together, but Jackie had a spirit about her that made me feel comfortable to be alone with her for an interview about Women of Alabaster. She was similar in build and age to me with a fluffy middle and substantial arms and legs. Her bright white hair was short and cropped at various lengths, which framed her tortoise-rimmed glasses and her kind, green eyes. We both have thinly shaped eyebrows that dated us long before the trendy wide, tattooed brows of today. Peeking out from her short-sleeved grey T-shirt was part of a large tattoo of some indistinguishable image. I withheld satisfying my curiosity until I heard her whole story. I was more focused on getting to know her personality and her purpose at Women of Alabaster. I learned that she serves as coordinator of the Cincinnati Day Center, and she has served in Scarlet's street ministry and as a Weekend Mama at Scarlet's Agape Farm. Quickly, I discovered Jackie's long history of being a servant for oppressed women and longed to hear more about her experiences.

Jackie was raised Catholic and heard of God, Jesus, and the Holy Spirit, but within the context of the sign of the cross that often begins and ends Catholic prayers. Beyond that, Jackie had not read the Bible, nor did her family own a Bible. Not much was spoken of God in the home, which was rather dysfunctional. Her mother was an alcoholic, and Jackie followed her mom's addiction into adulthood. Jackie became pregnant at age 18 when she was engaged and then got married.

Jackie's in-laws were Southern Baptists and not fond of having a Catholic daughter-in-law. "They didn't like my parents, and my parents did not like them. Our chaotic family life ended in divorce after a year and a half."

Said Jackie, "When I came back home, I came back with a '69 Buick, a baby on my hip, and seven dollars in my pocket. I had no job. I didn't go to college; I went right into being a wife and a mother. I lived with my parents for 3 years and got a job within the first two weeks at Cincinnati Bell. I was already drinking. I kept my job. Everything was going fine. Then I got my own place, my first apartment."

"My mom had my daughter more than I had my daughter because I was out every weekend until all hours doing all kinds of shenanigans: drinking and acting stupid. I went through a couple different jobs, due to circumstances with the merger of Cincinnati Bell and AT&T, then being laid off from AT&T when they sent everything overseas. They laid off 2,000 people in Cincinnati, and I was one of them."

Jackie went into the hair business because they paid her to go to school, so she did that for 25 years. She continued to drink and to stay completely away from the Lord. She put hair cutting to the side in order to care for her mother and grandmother, who died six months apart from each other. With no hair clientele to rebuild her salon business, Jackie looked for other employment and was advised by the hospice nurse to become a certified nurse's aide. She took the class for two weeks and worked with hospice for a year until the company disbanded. Then she worked for the supply house for beauticians and taught at the school. As a single mother, Jackie always worked more than one job. She had a daughter, a house payment, and an ex-husband who had nothing to do with her. He just left.

Jackie talked of her darkest moments. "Even though my family was dysfunctional, my parents were there for me and for my daughter. In 2015, I was still drinking and ended up having a nervous breakdown. I had a plan that I was going to kill myself. I told my best friend, who is a nurse. She left work to come and find me. I had my two grandkids with me, so she knew that it was important that she got to me. She took me to UC Hospital, and they put me in the psych ward for three days. I came out of there and knew that something had to change, so I started searching.

"I walked in darkness for a long time. The Lord delivered me from alcohol and cigarettes. I thought it was me; of course, years later, He told me it was Him. I started going to a church in 2015, and that's where I met Katie. I didn't understand why we became friends. I just didn't understand it."

Before Jackie was leaving on a mission trip to Africa, she visited Katie in the hospital. Katie said that she would have liked to go with the group. While Jackie was in Africa, Katie bought her a bracelet with elephants all the way around it from the hospital gift shop. Meanwhile, Jackie had brought Katie a bracelet from Africa. That exchange of bracelets solidified their friendship.

While Jackie and I shared our love of missions and our love for Africa, she lifted her right sleeve to show me her elephant tattoo that covered her entire upper arm and shoulder. The image was the outline of the country of Africa with a decorative elephant's head with flowers around its crown and the year 2018.

Then Jackie continued with her story about Katie. After seven months in the hospital, Katie was released from the hospital with no place to go. She called Jackie crying, "I don't know what to do. I don't know where I'm going to go."

Jackie responded, "You're coming here." Jackie put a cot in the living room of her one-bedroom apartment. Katie had to have heart surgery, and while she was staying with Jackie, Katie kept going back to her apartment, where she would relapse. She ended up in the hospital. She had been clean for 3 or 4 months.

Katie's apartment was on Vine Street, and she had an alley behind her that she called "Heroin Alley." If people were overdosing, they were knocking on her door. After she relapsed and was in the hospital, she called Jackie, "I don't know what to do."

Jackie took Katie back for a second time. She was on suboxone, so the two friends went every morning to get Katie suboxone; they went together to Katie's appointments with her heart doctor. With just the two of them in the room, the doctor said, "She has to stay on suboxone. This is what is going to keep you alive." Others had been telling Katie that she was just trading one drug for another. He said, "Once we do the surgery, when it's over, if you use one time, you're dead." He looked at Jackie and said, "Do you understand what I am saying?"

Jackie said, "Yes." She knew that the mother in her had to rise up. During Katie's heart surgery, some of her family members came to the hospital, where they sat and waited. Shortly after that, Katie stayed with Jackie for two weeks and then said that she had to get her own place. She wanted to be over by her brother's church. Her brother was Jackie's pastor. Katie found an apartment, and her brother and Jackie helped to move her into her apartment.

One day Katie was at Jackie's apartment sitting on her couch. She was at one end, and Katie was at the other. Jackie wanted to know Katie's whole story: how she ended up out on the streets doing drugs. Jackie hadn't done any of that and didn't know anybody who did.

As Katie and Jackie sat on the couch and talked, all of a sudden, Katie asked, "Have you ever heard of the Women of Alabaster?" Jackie had not. Then she asked, "Have you ever heard of Mama Scar?" No. Immediately Katie called Scarlet and said, "I think I have someone who wants to volunteer."

Doubts filled Jackie's mind. What was going on? She didn't know anything about drug addiction. She had been an alcoholic. She heard God saying to her, "Addiction is addiction is addiction." She was humbled to think that God had tapped her to befriend Katie. God had said to her, "This is why you are her friend. This is where I want you."

Jackie met Scarlet and started volunteering with her in the street ministry, which was totally new to her. Still walking with Katie a little bit through her recovery journey, Jackie came to the Cincinnati Day Center and started volunteering just on Thursdays until COVID hit. Then everything shut down.

Scarlet, Jackie, and other volunteers took turns leaving food and water, like bagged lunches, out by the door. The girls knew that food would be waiting for them outside the Day Center, because they were all calling Mama: "We're hungry. We don't know what's going on."

Scar said, "I'm going to have people bringing food down." Jackie wrote messages on the bags for the girls, and because of her friendship with Katie, she had developed a heart for all of the women. She felt that she had been so close to being out on the streets with them.

For three years. Jackie volunteered as a Weekend Mama for Scarlet's Agape Farm. Scarlet would stay at the farm Monday through Friday, Then the Weekend Mamas would come for the weekend to stay with the girls. It was a two-year program. They were learning how to step back into society: to do a checkbook and to just walk with the Lord. Eventually, the landlord needed the house back, but this was just a start for what Scarlet had in mind. They celebrated at least three girls, who graduated from that program.

Now Jackie runs the Cincinnati Day Center in Over The Rhine so that Scarlet can expand the ministries and Scarlet's vision for Women of Alabaster.

Jackie said that people have always prophesied over her, which led her to Women of Alabaster. Since 2015, different ministers and prophets have spoken words over Jackie that told her that she was going to help a lot of women.

In March 2024, two people prophesied over Jackie about Women of Alabaster, and when she attended a training session, she saw with clarity that she was to step in as coordinator of the Day Center. She left, crying all the way home and talking to God, saying, "I can't do it."

God said to her, "I have equipped you for this. What do you think you have been doing for five years?"

Jackie objected, "But I can't do what she does!"

God said, "I'm asking you to step in so she can go do what she has to do."

Humbly, Jackie went into Scarlet's office to tell her that she would take the position. Scarlet started laughing, and Jackie asked, "What are you laughing aboul?"

Scarlet said, "He already told me you were coming."

Prophetic Journal of Mama Scar:

> *To set apart - consecrate (key)*
>
> *Leviticus 22:21 Offerings accepted and not accepted and whoever offers a sacrifice of a peace offering to the Lord to fulfill his vow, or a freewill offering from the cattle or sheep, it must be perfect to be accepted. There shall be no defect in it.*

Psalm 4:3 But know that the Lord has set apart the godly for himself; the Lord hears when I call to him." Our lives lived for Christ is our setting apart ourselves to be set apart and different from the world (sin). We must live according to the "Word of Yahweh". When we fall into sin, we repent from our heart and ask the Lord to forgive us, turning away from what took us away from the Lord.

Each day we must consecrate the day to the Lord and put on the whole armor of Go to be able to withstand the tactics of the enemy. The enemy wants to deceive us and cause us to believe we are unforgiven and there is no sense in trying to stay set apart.

1 Timothy 2:5 "For there is one God, and one mediator between God and men, the man Christ Jesus."

But Jesus the only pure and holy sacrifice made it possible for us to come before a Holy God and stand robed in white and unblemished. Jesus is our Redeemer and we as believers remind ourselves daily of his goodness, mercy, love, and grace towards us.

Romans 5:8 The Word says that while we were yet sinners, Christ died for us. How can we not desire to be set apart and consecrated with and by Him.

1 John 1:9, it says, "If we confess our sins, He is faithful and just to forgive us our sins, and to cleanse us from all unrighteousness."

John 14:15 Jesus said if you love me, keep my commandments.

Luke 5:32 I came not to call the righteous, but sinners to repentance.

Luke 24:47 "And that repentance and remission of sins should be preached In His Name among all nations, beginning in Jerusalem."

Consecrate: the separation of oneself from things that are unclean, especially anything that would contaminate one's relationship with God, who is perfect.

Sanctification, Holiness, Purity

Joshua 3:5 Consecrate yourselves for tomorrow the Lord will do amazing things among You.

NOTE: Israelites entering the Promised Land - Commence and Promise

Prophetic Journal of Mama Scar:

2/18/2022

You are here, Lord, in the midst of us, loving us, healing us. Glory is shining all around You, Lord. Your daughters hear Your voice and answer You beckoning. Beckon us, Oh Lord. We are in Your Holy Holy Presence, Lord. We are so in awe of You, oh Lord. Most Holy Lord, Most Holy Lord. - Change us, Lord.

Chapter 7

"Forgiveness isn't for the other person." - Mary

Mary's childhood was negatively impacted by her family's history of suicide, molestation, and other mental illnesses. She was taught to do good or she would go to hell in a fire and brimstone Baptist theology. Within a seven month period, Mary's grandpa shot himself in the head with a full .44 magnum; her grandmother took a whole bottle of heart pills; and her mother's boyfriend raped her. Her mother, suffering from paranoid schizophrenia, believed the rapist and told Mary that she was a whore. Mary was 11. She didn't even know what that meant.

At age 11, Mary went into foster care, where she grew up and eventually became pregnant.

Mary met her "first big trick," who lived in a different country. Mary was working in a store on Harrison Avenue in Cincinnati, when the owner suggested that she write to his son. Her boss flew Mary to Aman, Jordan, with the intent of helping the son get to the United States. Mary fell in love with the culture and the people of Aman. She was there by herself with the owner's Muslim family. Mary had been raised Christian Baptist and did not convert to Muslim, but she enjoyed seeing the land where Jesus walked, even though she did not feel a relationship with Jesus. She saw the Dead Sea, the Red Sea, Mount Nebo, Petra, and Aqaba. She never realized that the trip was a trick, and her intended one month stay turned into 19 months. The owner's son would give her anything she asked for, but as she says, not all money is good money.

When she returned from Jordan, Mary met a drug addict and developed a relationship with him. While high, he accidentally tripped over one of her children, causing injury, Children Services investigated and removed the children from the home. At 24, Mary, distraught, filled the void with drugs. Mary's children were put in the custody of her grandmother, the only person who had ever shown Mary any kind of affection or love. When her grandmother died of breast cancer, the children went to foster care, but Mary stayed with her man. Besides abusing drugs, he was actually prostituting himself. Then he became her abuser for the next 15 years on the streets of Cincinnati. Mary says of those years, "I was trying to die every day."

Mary met Mama Scar 12 years ago, but Mary saw Scarlet as this annoying woman who would not leave her alone. Mary was just trying to get high and trying to survive the street life. However, Scarlet kept telling her, "Jesus loves you."

And for probably five years, Mary told Mama Scar, "Jesus wasn't talking about women like me!"

Scarlet would respond, "Oh, yes, He is! You will know when it's time!"

The first time she got clean, Mary stayed sober for 18 months before a relapse. She called Mama Scar again and said, "Come and get me. I'm on the block. I don't know what the f*** I'm doing. Come and get me and take me to jail. I want to go to jail. I don't need this."

Through that process, Mary got to know Mama, the women, and ultimately, the plan that God has for her life. She has been sober for 6 years and is one of the clinical staff at the Hamilton County Justice Center working for the Addictions Services Council. Mary also has her CDCA and Peer Recovery Support License for the state of Ohio.

About Mama Scar, Mary said, "I help women who are involved in sex trafficking, or human trafficking, in any way that I can. It was all from the seed that Mama Scar planted. She has always been there for me, through everything, everything, even on the street. I could call her, and I remember one morning, I called her at 5:00 a.m., and I said, 'He beat me up, and he took my shoes, and I'm out here. I have no shoes, and it's freezing.' And she was there to get me…with no shoes on. She put me in the car, brought me to the building (that wasn't even open yet–it didn't open until 10), brought me inside to get warm, and let me get a shower. She has done this on numerous occasions.

"I WAS these women. That's why it's important for me to come back, because she knew His plan a long time ago. What she does is really important because there are a lot of women out there who don't know that they have a choice. It's important for us to give back so that they know that they don't have to keep living like that. That's why I give back."

Since being sober, Mary has lost about 30 friends. She lost both her parents to cancer within 15 months of each other. Mary is grateful that she was able to be her parents' caregivers while she was sober, and she was able to help them transition.

Mary said, "I really think that forgiveness isn't for the other person. Forgiveness is for me. If I'm resentful and I hold on to all this pain and anger and shame and guilt and everything that has kept me sick for so long, then that's like drinking poison and expecting somebody else to die. I'm a very rational, logical person. I believe that what you put out is what you get, so how can I go in here and show these women how to heal if I haven't healed myself. It's not possible. That's Mama's goal. Wellness. The goal is to bring people closer to God, to show them that they don't have to be defined by their terrible choices. We can still surround ourselves with this beautiful community that she has created."

Katie has been Mary's best friend since they got high together on the street. They got sober three months apart. Now they come to the Cincinnati Day Center for a couple hours each week in hopes that they can catch somebody and connect them with treatment. The two friends also work together. Presently, Mary works as a clinician with a pod of 18 women. Katie does the coordination when people are actually getting out of jail; her desk is right there by the door, so when they're released, she's the first person they see. Katie talks to everybody when they come out, and that's what they need. Said Mary of their work: "The women need to know that there is a choice. That's why we're here. We might not always make the right choice, but when we have the right people around us and the right people supporting us, it's easier to make the right choice."

Mary has had the opportunity of working with the Ohio Justice and Policies Center to get her entire record sealed under the Safe Harbor Expungement for victims of sex trafficking. Her total record included 197 charges, 11 felony convictions, and two prison numbers. The Ohio Justice and Policies Center for Second Chance Program has used Mary's success story in their fundraiser to help other women. Mary says, "I know that I am in a minority of women with success, so I have to be here to do this."

Mary's thoughts match Scarlet's philosophy. Mary explained, "We're not here to push them; we're here to plant seeds. That's it. And that's what Mama did for me. That's all she did. She planted the seed, and she showed up. That's the two most important things to do: show up and plant seeds. You listen; you show up; and you tell them that they have a choice. Those three simple things can change someone's whole life trajectory! Then eventually you let them know that they are worthy and that Jesus loves them and that God loves them. Even though I believe what I believe, I am not necessarily able to talk about God like that all the time because of my profession. There are ethical boundaries that I can't cross, but I can tell them what worked for me. It's OK if they don't believe in God. I didn't, either. I can give them the tools that I used. I think it's important to meet everyone where they are, just like Mama Scar has always done."

On Mary's arm is a colorful tattoo that reads, "Beauty for Ashes," and another that reads: "She made broken look beautiful and strong look invincible. She walked with the universe on her shoulders and made it look like a pair of wings." The second is a quote that her daughter sent to her when she first got sober. In addition, Mary has a tattoo of her mother and father and a tattoo on her neck that covers her track marks from drugs. The tattoo is a delicate tree with colorful vines growing up toward Mary's face.

Mary's face today is full of peace and joy. She beams when she speaks of her work at Women of Alabaster and the Justice Center. Her way of giving back and showing gratitude is to reach out to other women to offer recovery and hope.

Prophetic Journal of Mama Scar:
2/21/2022

To Execute 1 Kings 5:9

To execute a decree - to do what is provided or required
Follow out or through - to perform, to inflict
To execute judgment or vengeance
To effect, carry into complete effect, to finish
To pursue to the end

1 Kings 5:9 NKJV Prepare to build my temple (Get Ready)

My servants shall bring them down from Lebanon to the sea; I will float them in rafts by the sea to the place you indicate to me, and will have them broken apart there, then you can take them away. And you shall <u>fulfill</u> my desire by giving food for my household.

Yahweh can and will use even the enemies (unbelievers) to complete His Will. King Hiram of Tyre was a type of unbeliever with a need, and Solomon was able to fulfill his father David's desire to build the temple.

The cedars of Lebanon is a tree planted by Yahweh (Ps. 104:16 Is 41:19) They are strong and durable. Is. 9:10 graceful and beautiful (Ps. 80:10, Ezekiel 17:23) high and tall (Amos 2:9, Ez. 17:22) fragrant (song of Songs 4:11) and spreading wide. We are to be like the cedar, strong and we the remnant are a sign of strength and eternity. Yahweh made us to last, to endure and to fulfill His Plan.

To transport and harvest. The trees had to cut through steep mountains, split rocks, construct a road, and build a way to transport on the Mediterranean Sea.

Remnant Tree Cedars - we stand tall and we have large massive hearts. We love the Lord, our God, and therefore, we love His people. We have irregular heads like the cedar. The head of cedar has many branches on the heading. We, too, have many branches on our head, holds our brain with all our life experiences. Each experience will have power over us, some good and some bad. But the remnant knows who controls the head/mind. Ephesians tells us we have the mind of Christ; the Bible also tells us to take every thought captive unto God. We have the strength and ability to be and live the fulfilled life Yahweh planned for us when we continuously give our head over to God.

Young cedars have smooth dark bark that turns brown, that gets fissured and scaly with age. Remnant, we must age with Yahweh leading us from Glory to Glory to Glory. We must not allow aging and one life experience to darken our youthful exuberance for the Lord.

The leaves of the cedar are needle-like, three-sided, rigid leaves are scattered along long shoots and clustered in tufts at the end of short spurs. Remnant, the needle-like leaves remind me of the need to protect itself, like we protect ourselves with the Word of Yahweh against the fiery darts of the enemy - the three-sided leaves remind me of the Holy Trinity: Father, Son, and Holy Spirit.

Each of the leaves of the cedar has 2 resin canals and these remain on the tree for 3 to 6 years. Remnant, we are fed by 2 canals as well; running through us is the Blood of Christ and the Power of the Holy Spirit. All we need is contained in these 2 canals. Rivers of LIving Water flowing continually cleansing us, purifying the Bride of Christ for His Return.

Remnant, the 3 to 6 years the canals remain on the tree sent me to the meaning of numbers. #3 Resurrection, Divine completeness, Perfection, Godhead/Trinity. #6 Man's number, Satan, His Influence, 3+6=9 Fruit of the Spirit, Divine Completeness. From the

Lord 3+6+9=18 which represents bondage.

Remnant, if we allow our spiritual canals to dry up, we can see how we could become in bondage to the enemy. As the cedars need these two reasons to live, we must have the Trinity at work in us at all times. Otherwise, we become spiritually dead and lost for the world.

Break the rafts apart as you can take them away!! The Lord is breaking and shaking the Remnant to allow them to leave all the worldly attachments behind so He can carry them into the Promised Land. Otherwise, how can we share the truth (the Gospel) with those still away from Yahweh.

We are rebuilding the 3rd Temple, as Yahweh's children and preparing ourselves for the Return of Yahweh. We must be ready. The time for "What if" is over; no more running away from hard things. Come out of hiding, remnant.

Psalm 69 references Yeshua and talks about his jealous defense of His Holy Worship. 69:9 For the zeal of Your house has eaten Me up, and the reproaches of those who reproached You have fallen upon Me.

Chapter 8

"Taste, Texture, & Technique"
— Sister NayNay

Sister NayNay stood at the stove in the kitchen of the Cincinnati Day Center of Women of Alabaster, preparing a plate of hot food for a woman seated at the table in layers of well worn clothing and tattered shoes. Another woman sat at the table with one foot in a bucket as Mama Scar filled the bucket with warm water and lightly massaged the woman's swollen leg. The conversation was light and lively. The aroma from the trays of barbecued ribs mixed with the sight of large homemade iced cinnamon rolls drew my attention back to the stove and Sister NayNay. Her hands never stopped preparing and serving the food while she chatted with the other women. Her broad smile and beautiful white teeth almost outshined the sparkling crystals that completely covered her baseball style hat. Through the kitchen window, bright sunbeams danced to deflect the depressing view of the urban neighborhood with its graffitied walls and dilapidated sidewalks. This was not merely a soup kitchen in an almost abandoned building in Cincinnati. This was a professional chef's canvas of love, and her masterpiece was the plate of delicious food served with kindness, warmth, and care. To the women coming in from the streets, this was a five-star restaurant in a fast food neighborhood.

I was reminded of the book of Daniel 12:2-3:

2 Multitudes who sleep in the dust of the earth will awake: some to everlasting life, others to shame and everlasting contempt. 3 Those who are wise will shine like the brightness of the heavens, and those who lead many to righteousness, like the stars for ever and ever. NIV

Sister NayNay is such a shining star for the Women of Alabaster. Her birth name is Alicia Renee Jackson, but her family calls her by her middle name, Renee. Mama Scar lovingly calls her "Sister NayNay." Scarlet and Renee first connected at the BP gas station on Madison Road in Cincinnati. Renee went inside to get coffee and saw a group buying soft drinks. She noticed that a young girl was attempting to purchase all of their soft drinks with food stamps, but the gas station attendant would not take her food stamp card. Seeing the disappointment on the girl's face, Renee offered to buy the drinks for them. This gesture prompted a conversation with the group's leaders, Jim Turner and his wife. They had been on their way to do street outreach ministry but had gotten lost off the Norwood Lateral and stopped for refreshments. Renee took his card and said that she wanted to join them in their outreach ministry.

With the group called the Dream Center, Renee started preparing food on Monday nights and taking it with her. What started as a little pot of chili and some hot cocoa grew into a massive spread of food. And what started as a handful of people grew to a larger group with Scarlet and people from the Church on Fire. Scarlet and Renee became good friends, serving together for years until Scarlet began Women of Alabaster. Renee became Scarlet's food partner, Sister NayNay, first at the location on McMickan Street and then at the present location on Central Avenue.

Sister NayNay said of the ministry, "There is love in the house. There is love in this place. If you come here, you will be loved on. You will be prayed for. You will be blessed. You will be ministered to. This is a safe place. That is what keeps me here. This safe place and the love that is shown from everybody. We all have different personalities, but everybody shows love, even the ladies that come in, the ones that we minister to, because they had lives; they had kids; they had husbands. There but by the grace of God go I. I love to be able to share and have them enjoy the food, the company, the fellowship, and to know that they look forward to Monday.

"They ask, 'Is Sister NayNay going to be there? Sister NayNay, are you going to be there?'

"I will always answer, 'I'm coming! I'm coming!'"

Renee used to work at UC Hospital in the dietary department. She worked there until her three children decided whether or not they wanted to go to school for free. At that time, employees' kids could go to school for free. When she turned 40, Renee resigned from there and started her own barbeque business in Madisonville. Then she switched to baking rolls to sell at Findlay Market. The first day she sold 30 dozen rolls in two hours.

Learning to cook from her mother, Renee has her own business baking breads and desserts and has been selling them at Findlay Market for almost 20 years. She works all weekends selling a variety of baked goods: bread pudding, peach cobbler, blueberry pies, blackberry cobbler, apple cobbler, sweet potato pie, cranberry pumpkin bread, whole wheat zucchini bread, whole wheat banana bread, yeast rolls, jalapeño bread, cheese and garlic bread, sundried tomato....

As Renee listed all of her menu items, my mouth started to water and my mind drifted to my childhood memories of my mother's good cooking. Food is such a sensory memory for people, so women walking in from stark circumstances to Renee's aromatic cuisine most likely take her little bit of heaven with them in their memories.

Renee's mom worked as a supervisor in a nursing home and cooked in their kitchen for years. She also cooked all the time for the church. They called her "Ms. Jackson." Renee learned to cook from her mother, never using recipes. Renee said, "It's technique. There's a difference. I don't know how much she put in, but I go by taste, technique, and texture." Renee's business is called "NayNay's."

When some friends were having issues getting around and getting food during the Pandemic, Renee started a non-profit for people 65 and over, called "Cooking for the King." Every Friday, customers get three free meals from her organization. She doesn't deliver. She sends a menu out on Monday and expects orders by Wednesday. Her customers were friends with sick husbands, friends who didn't cook, friends with cancer, and friends in the hospital with six other people at home. Renee says that she doesn't turn anyone away, but the guidelines say 65 and over. She would like to grow to being able to deliver the meals, but presently she is the only cook with the volunteers who help her.

Renee's favorite memory at Women of Alabaster is a girl named Debbie. Women were standing in a circle praying for Debbie. As Renee prayed, she could literally see a transformation in her. Debbie completely relaxed, and her face changed in that moment. Renee and Debbie connected. As reports came in when Debbie would come in and out of the Day Center, Renee would hear her saying, "I'm doing this. I'm not doing this...."

Renee would think, "OK, God, you're doing your thing." Renee saw Debbie a couple months ago at the church; she was looking well, still doing her "stuff," but looking much better.

Said Renee: "I just think about her all the time. She is one of the most memorable for me. There are just so many memorable times here. I've been here with

Women of Alabaster for over 10 years. I never get tired of it, but there are days when I am tired."Mary's face today is full of peace and joy. She beams when she speaks of her work at Women of Alabaster and the Justice Center. Her way of giving back and showing gratitude is to reach out to other women to offer recovery and hope.

Prayer Journal of Mama Scar:

2/27/2022

My thoughts: All things begin and end with the Lord…

★ *Beginning anything starts with prayer to the Father, which must be constant during the middle of any daily living, life changes and ministry. Otherwise, we may get off course by thinking we know best or others' opinions are necessary for the outcome of any and all life choices we make.*

But we see in all the scriptures prayers, relationship, and time with the Father is the beginning and end of all our life. Yahweh invites us to come up to the Throne Room and get our instruction for each day.

★ *If we are to finish strong in our journey with and for the Lord, we must begin and end each day with Him.*

Who are we to assume we can do anything without Him? He can accomplish more in 1 second than we without Him can in 1 year.

Activation:

STOP PRAY AM & PM Deut. 6:4-5

Listen for instruction

Bring petitions to Him

Go to the Word for instruction

Worship Him, praise Him, invite Him

Enter into relationship with Him and ask His opinion before asking others

Look for His hand to direct you throughout the day, if you become frustrated or confused (STOP-PRAY-LISTEN-MOVE FORWARD)

Chapter 9

"Self-forgiveness is a lifelong journey." — Esther

Some women carry the signs of their former street lives in their faces, posture, demeanor, or voices. Esther does not. Whatever she may still keep in her memory or heart, Esther presents herself with a sense of confidence, professionalism, and positivity. Her light brown hair reflected the light and framed her face. I could see large silver hoop earrings peeking out from her hair. She had a glow about her, perhaps from her subdued makeup, but more likely from her broad smile. Complementing her trim, athletic figure, Esther wore a white turtleneck sweater with grey stripes, tight blue jeans accented by a leather rhinestone belt with a large western buckle, and brown knee-high leather boots. She set her black leather tote on the chair and greeted me warmly. I admired her attention to detail as I noticed her French manicured nails with thin raspberry colored tips.

Esther was gracious to take time from her work schedule to meet with me. As she brushed into the room past Scarlet's desk to take a seat next to me, she spoke quickly and perhaps a bit nervously. However, as she settled into our interview, she seemed to relax and put thoughts of her work responsibilities aside to tell her story.

Like other women that I have interviewed, Esther went through a tough childhood and even tougher life on the street, but her summary of her success today will stay with me for a long time. In a world where many people see themselves as victims without ever taking control over their lives, Esther refuses to see herself as a victim. I could put her words on a poster and frame it for myself: "We always have the opportunity to rewrite our narrative. Nobody should feel discarded. We are all resilient beings that have priceless worth. No matter what circumstance we find ourselves in, we can rise above it and come out. I know I am not a victim of anything or anyone. I made a lot of bad choices, but those choices do not define who I am today. The scars I have tell a story of determination, perseverance, and survival. I will continue to share who I am and hope other people will realize that they, too, have an opportunity to find freedom."

When Esther was 12 years old, her little sister died at Children's Hospital when she was only 27 days old. Understandably, the family suffered terribly from the loss. Esther's anxiety escalated as did her parents' anger and tension. No one talked about their feelings. She was taught never to talk to anyone else about what went on at home. In those days, mental health really wasn't addressed.

For Esther, school was a daily nightmare. She remembers waking up and thinking, "Oh, God, I have to do this again today." Before a test, she would panic and nearly vomit. She was in advanced classes, so she would get high before school to be able to stay calm and focus better in class. She had access to drugs through friends. Once she realized that she liked using, that is how she made friends. Esther said, "If they were able to provide what I needed, then they were my friends. I lost sight of all my goals at that time. I started using things like marijuana, acid, alcohol, and pills. I tried to get high enough to be able to breathe, to talk, and to be funny. I could relax and feel less anxious about everything. I thought I was partying, but I was self-medicating."

By age 19, she was hooked on heroin and exposed to everything that comes along with a drug lifestyle. When she was 22 or 23, she started smoking crack cocaine. That is when she was introduced to the street lifestyle and the sex trade. She only interacted with people doing drugs, selling drugs, or licks (johns). Esther said, "I felt invisible and worthless, like I wasn't human anymore. I didn't allow myself to get close to people, which was how I survived. The longer I stayed out there, the lower my standards got. I stopped being able to recognize who I was before I started getting high and hustling.

"I lived a street lifestyle for over a decade. I was exposed to a lot of very harsh experiences. I've seen a lot. I had things done to me. It is a war zone out there. That's a subculture with its own set of rules and its own set of laws. I experienced a lot of trauma just from that. I developed a hard shell. A street minister named Rich was the first to break that hard shell."

On a Sunday, Mother's Day, hustling was slow; money was low; and Esther was sad because she and the other women weren't included as a part of the holiday, or any holidays, for that matter. Even though Pastor Rich doesn't smoke or believe in smoking, he had bought a pack of cigarettes and was giving them to the moms on the street. The only reason Esther spoke to him is because she needed a cigarette or two. When she sat down on the curb, she was surprised that he sat down with her.

Esther said, "I thought, wow! He actually is sitting on the ground with me. I thought that was kind of cool because he didn't think he was better than me. We just started having a conversation, and I remember thinking how kind he was. I didn't really encounter a lot of kind people in my environment."

Pastor Rich and Esther developed a friendship, and he would take her to do what she called "normal things." A highlight was their trip to the Aronoff Center to see a documentary film on natural miracles and to meet Scarlet Hudson.

Another girl with them had met Scarlet before and said, "Oh, you're going to love her. She is so cool and so pretty." Esther learned that Scarlet worked in the hairstyling business. Esther was attracted to Scarlet's beautifully manicured nails, high heels, and the way she was dressed "to the nines." Esther had grown up seeing women dressed like her, but life and dress on the street (or "on the block" as she called it) was completely different.

Esther described her first impression of Scarlet: "I will always remember the first moment when we met. Scarlet embraced me and hugged me and didn't appear shocked or turned off by my appearance. When I was using drugs, I didn't care what I looked like and wouldn't change my clothes for days. Scarlet seemed to care more about me than I cared about myself. She smiled like she was truly happy to see me. She said, 'Oh, it's so good to meet you,' and I knew that she sincerely meant it."

Esther saw Scarlet periodically through her outreach efforts and the community of Over The Rhine. She was volunteering with a community outreach ministry, called the Dream Center. They would come out and would provide food, prayer, warm blankets, and necessities. By the time Women of Alabaster was established, Esther had gotten clean. However, the ministry was a huge part of her recovery.

Esther felt extremely uncomfortable transitioning from the street subculture to living in conventional society. Scarlet provided a safe haven, not just for those women who were using, but for those who were in recovery. During one of her darkest moments, Esther was in deep emotional pain, sobbing and struggling not to get high when she received a call from her friend, who was in recovery and thriving. Esther confessed that she was not doing so well and didn't know why she was on Elm Street Her friend directed Esther to go straight to Scarlet, who was right down the street at the Day Center. Esther's friend stayed on the phone with her until she arrived.

Walking into Scarlet's office, Esther looked at Scarlet and slumped into a chair. No words transpired between them. Esther started sobbing from the pit of her stomach as Scarlet knelt at her feet, putting her hands on Esther's knees. She didn't say anything. Esther recalled, "She just let me sob, just a painful sob until I stopped, and I felt peace. I'm pretty sure she was praying over me, but she wasn't doing it out loud. We never spoke, but that night I did not give into temptation, and when I left the building, I had no desire to get high. That would not have happened like that without God, my friend's phone call, and Women of Alabaster (Scarlet).

"What I know today is that God will always provide a way out for us; we just have to be willing to take it. I was willing that day. We never spoke about what happened. Scarlet does not put pressure on me to talk about my feelings unless that is what I want to do. I believe that God placed people, like Rich and Scar, in my life because he knew he had a purpose and a plan for me. Even though I didn't know at the time, nor did I feel worthy, God has his final say."

At 35 years of age, Esther got sober and turned her attention toward furthering her education. With a friend, who was also in recovery, Esther started school at Cincinnati State to earn her CDCA in the Addiction Study Program. When Esther's laptop broke, Scarlet allowed her to access her personal "fancy" laptop with a touch screen. She let Esther take it home to complete assignments. Said Esther, "I remember feeling so privileged that she trusted me with her laptop. She was one of the first people to actually trust me. My friend and I were also able to go to her office to work in peace."

Esther only had suitable clothing for serving tables at a restaurant, so when Esther acquired her first professional job, Scarlet was there to help. She made sure that Esther had an entire wardrobe of business casual clothing. Presently, Esther works in a program with trafficking survivors that are also interested in substance abuse treatment. She has also been promoted and has served in various capacities.

Scarlet continues to be a spiritual mentor for Esther through her sobriety. Esther's sobriety date is April 16, 2014.

Esther speaks highly of Scarlet. "I have never met anybody like Scarlet, other than my grandmother, and I think that is what has drawn me so close to her, why I was able to trust her so newly in sobriety. My grandmother was a devout woman of God. I miss being able to call her for guidance, but I can count on

Scarlet to guide me in any situation, including parenting advice for my son. In fact, my son adores Scarlet and refers to her as "Aunt Scarlet." Before she died, my grandmother did get to see me sober for a short period of time and got to meet my son. Scarlet and my grandmother actually say the same things! I will say to Scarlet, 'That's what Nonny has told me my whole life!' I can receive it differently now because I'm more mature, and because I have my own personal relationship with God. I'm not afraid to receive the truth.

"Scarlet pours Scripture into me and all the women she serves. She shows us the love of Jesus through consistent actions of love and kindness. The best way to encourage someone is to use the words that come straight from God. If you know Scarlet, you know that she will always bring Scripture to the conversation, and she takes the time to teach you what the Scripture means.

"Self-forgiveness is a lifelong journey. I get the privilege of being a part of situations that teach me forgiveness. I get a different perspective of myself from the work that I do. I never thought that it would give me so much personally. I wanted to give back and do something that I believed in. Of course, I need to work for financial reasons, but I get the privilege of doing what I believe in. Ironically, it has become a huge part of my healing process. As I work with these women, I get to hear their stories, and I get to watch them set goals and accomplish them. I get to watch the light come on in their eyes, and they start to walk with their heads up. I get to see hope. There are so many things that I am doing that I never thought that I would be doing or that I would even want to do."

Today Esther has healthy goals: to heal, to find peace, to raise her son, and to go back to college for a degree in social work. As I listened to Esther describe her feelings and emotions through the traumatic times of her life, I was impressed at the growth that she has shown. From a child in a home of suppressed feelings to an adult in a career of helping others to process their feelings, Esther has shown incredible resilience and determination to remain emotionally stable. She is breaking the cycle of trauma, not only for her and her son, but for all the women who will be learning from her in the future

Prayer Journal of Mama Scar:

8/24/2021

Prayer for Divine Alignment

Father God, in the name of Jesus,

I thank you for divine alignment in the Spirit. I declare that I am vertically and horizontally lined up with the will of Yahweh. The blood of the

everlasting covenant of Jesus Christ covers me. It has made me perfect in every good work. (Hebrews 13:21) I am standing on the foundation of Christ. I am laying for myself a good foundation for the future that I may have eternal life. (1 Timothy 6:19)

I will not be pulled to and fro because I am maturing daily in the things of Yahweh (Eph 4:14). I live in the Rhema, and it is activating signs, wonders, and miracles around me on a normal basis. Surely goodness and mercy have my back all the days of my life. (Psalms 23:6). Because I have divine sonship, I will abide on the course of the Lord and not be led astray. I stand at the Ascent of Ziz! This is my season and my place to blossom. I am under divine alignment of the heavenlies... All connections to the second heaven are dismantled. Every prince or ruler operating against my destiny is dethroned. The Lord has commanded the stars to fight the enemies of their path over me. (Judges 5:20) No weapon formed against me will prosper.

Lord, bless me indeed. Let there be no question that you are working on my behalf. The anointing of the mega is my portion. Lord, You have brought me a long way, and Your hand is on all that concerns me. I thank You for enlarging my coast. Keep me from evil so that my spirit will not be grieved or my soul pushed out of alignment.

Jesus, I praise You because I can see the place of my tent enlarged.. The curtains of my habitation are stretched forth, and I will spare not and will lengthen cords and strengthen my stakes. I am breaking forth on every side, and my seed shall inherit the Gentiles and make desolate cities inhabited. I have no fear, and I will not be damned, cursed, or confounded. The shame of my past and the reproach of my widowhood are cast into the sea of forgetfulness forever. Amen.

Chapter 10

"God gets it right." — Trudy

$\mathcal{T}$rudy remembers sitting in church at 7 or 8 years old when the windows were open, a beautiful breeze was blowing in, and everybody was singing hymns. It was such a moment of joy. All that she could think was, "Jesus!" "Jesus!" Now she understands that Jesus is in the music, as Psalm 22:3 says, "God inhabits our praise." Trudy's love of music caused her to take piano lessons. Her piano teacher also taught her three basic chords on the guitar, so Trudy was able to add her own singing voice to many 3-chord songs. After high school, Trudy studied music at Indiana State, and she now plays strings, violin, cello, and some of the "fat brass sounds for those rocky tunes." Although she plays worship music for her church, Trudy is a nurse and worked at Tri-Health.

Trudy's love for music and people shows. She accompanies kids in a band while they learn to play together on their own. "We're in church on Sunday night, and we've got a big praise band in this little bitty town of Rising Sun, Indiana. We're growing, and we got a new young minister. People are making decisions. People are getting to know God. People are getting to know Jesus. I've been working with the young people who want to be in the praise band. I'm teaching one young man to play the keyboard, and he says that he's going to replace me one day. Isn't that wonderful? One day he is going to replace me."

Trudy's outward appearance was distinctly unique from all the other women that I have met through Women of Alabaster. She sported no makeup, no tattoos, no jewelry, no stylish coiffure. Her face showed some signs of aging with just a few crinkles rather than wrinkles with the healthy glow of a school girl from Midwestern suburbia. Her unassuming demeanor was accented by her straight light brown hair parted in the middle and sitting comfortably below her shoulders. Her light green eyes were framed by rounded wire-rimmed glasses. She advertised no messages or sponsorship on her plain grey T-shirt over a heather maroon, long-sleeve cotton shirt. Extending from the cuffs of her shirt were her hands with a couple of blue veins that tattled on her age, but her long, slim fingers were a sign of her musical talent. Her hands rested on plain blue jeans. From head to toe, this slim figure of a woman exuded comfort, peace, calm, joy, and humility. A lover of Jesus, music, and nursing, Trudy is a perfect fit to serve women from the streets, which she has been doing for the past year.

When Scarlet came to Trudy's church to speak about Women of Alabaster, it was the first time that the two of them had met, even though Rising Sun Church of Christ in Rising Sun, Indiana had been supporting WOA for maybe five years. As Scarlet spoke, God was telling Trudy that this was something that he wanted her to do. For Trudy, it was the most apparent moment in her life that God had spoken directly to her. She approached Scarlet after the service and hugged her saying, "You're going to be hearing from me."

Immediately, Trudy went into Walmart with the list of needs for the day ministry. On the list was small and medium sized ladies' underwear, and Walmart had a tremendous box of packages of small and medium ladies' underwear for $2.00 each. Trudy felt that they had been right there waiting on her. (I always refer to this as "spiritual shopping.") Trudy started making casseroles to feed the women. She would drive up SR 262 to Dillosboro to take food and items to the barber shop where Scarlet's husband (Bob the Barber) worked. Scarlet sent her emails and updates on the ministry. .

A second time, God spoke to Trudy regarding the ministry, saying, "You're not quite there." When Trudy found out about the need for backpacks, she told Scarlet that it might be possible to supply 6 or 8, maybe 10 backpacks. However, the floodgates opened as her church supplied over 40 fully stocked backpacks last year.

Trudy said, "You begin to think about these women being out on the streets, and you can see what would be really good: chapstick and hygiene products. Every one of those backpacks were full: Chef Boyardee in a bag with a spoon, candy, lotions, body wash, wet wipes, hand warmers, gloves, scarves, and hats, even blankets."

When Scarlet expressed a need for volunteers in Over The Rhine area at the Day Center, Trudy accepted the call. Trudy described how she feels about her work there: "Blessings have just washed down over me, and I know they are from the Holy Spirit. I know that God sends that to me. In that respect, I don't know that I have ever been happier."

The biggest blessing of her day was getting to ring the bell because one of the girls went to treatment. Tears flowed from Trudy's face as she gave thanks to God for moving in the life of one of the girls. "I know that it doesn't work always, you know. It's a long road, and I know that there's a young woman out there that I wish I could just grab her up and make her go, but I can't do that. That doesn't work, but I keep talking and I keep praying. In their time and in God's time, I think God gets it right."

From her work as a nurse and personally, Trudy understands addiction, the draw that it has on people, and the long road to recovery. The beginning of that road to recovery is unconditional love, rest, a hot meal, a new outfit, a shower, and community support. Trudy loves watching the gradual transformation when it works.

"The most memorable woman was the one young woman who came in who had been beaten up badly. I don't think she was from the streets. I don't think she ever came back actually. I never saw anybody with that much bruising on her face. When she came in, she was feeling really defeated. Her face was really, really bad. We talked and we prayed and we cried. She got a shower and a new outfit. When she came out, she looked totally different. Her body language went from defeat to 'Ok, I've got another day now. I'm going to go out here and see what goes.' It was her first and last visit. She never came back." Trudy still thinks about her and prays for her.

Another memory is of a young woman who came in and wanted to eat right away. She said that she had not eaten in a long while. Trudy thought this was unusual because the downtown Cincinnati area has multiple locations for people to get food. She had never seen anybody eat quite that fast. Trudy wondered if the woman had any idea where she was going to get her next meal. Moments like these make Trudy cry.

"Keep loving them, take care of their needs, their basic, daily needs so that they can live for this day, and they know that they can come back on Wednesday, and then again next Monday. This time of year scares me a little bit because of the cold weather. It's hard; it's cold. It frightens me, but doesn't frustrate me. There is hope. There is hope with Women of Alabaster. There is love. There are some daily needs that we can cover. There is always hope, and with God, nothing is impossible. With patience and waiting for him on his timing, as the Bible tells us to do, we must be patient and let God do what he's supposed to do. There is hope here. There is hope here. It happens. And when you see it, it's beautiful. Within this three hour time period, you can see change happen. I believe that Scarlet is an angel. She is an angel. That's just the way it is."

Prayer Journal of Mama Scar:

7/28/2021

Ephesians 2:10 Created to do good things

We are His masterpiece.

Created us in Christ Jesus NEW

Do the works - to walk in them.

Every person was created to do good things.

Every person has a ministry and every person is a minister.

Acts 9:36-41 Tabitha (Dorcas)

Take what you're good at and use it to do good things. You don't do good things because you feel unqualified.

Someone's opinion of you does not have to become your reality. You don't have to be great to get started, but you do have to get started to do something great.

You don't do good things because you feel unqualified.

Galatians 1:13-15

He uses imperfect people because there are no perfect people. Every saint has a past, and every sinner has a future.

Chapter 11

"Hey, God! Next time..."
— Nora

*I*f I told you Nora's age, you wouldn't believe me. She is a young looking, vibrant brunette with long, wavy hair, matching deep brown eyes, peachy complexion, and a demure smile highlighted by the perfect shade of red to complement her bright pink blouse. Peeking out of her locks were long, feathery earrings that almost touched her open linked gold chain around her wrinkle free neck. Because I own a mirror, I always notice the necks of women over 30 to see how they disguise the effects of gravity and loose skin. Nora has beauty secrets that she did not share with me. After hearing her story, I am even more amazed that she effuses such a positive attitude on life, which shows through in her natural beauty and charm.

Her trauma began in her childhood from being raised by both of her biological parents on the west side of Cincinnati. They drank and fought a lot. Nora was determined not to be like them. She never smoked cigarettes or drank alcohol, but anger, depression, and anxiety weighed her down. When she was 11 or 12 years old, she began to sneak a can of Hudepohl Gold for herself when she fetched one for her father. The beer gave her a release from the lifestyle she was living, and her cycle of drinking escalated.

At the age of 14, she was drinking one night and was raped by a stranger, an older man. Then he dragged her down the street. She woke up in the hospital, and the man got arrested. Her parents didn't believe in psychiatrists or therapy, and they didn't go to church. There was no support, and she was left to deal with her trauma on her own. She became suicidal after that; she became a cutter. She would hurt herself and hide it, trying to cover up her pain.

She couldn't understand why rape had happened to her. Why was her life so hard? Comparing herself to the other children in school did not help either. She became very ill and delved into hard drugs and alcohol. Her parents warned her to stop or she would have to leave their home.

Nora left home at 15 with what she called a huge, gaping hole inside of her. Empty and lost, she developed a hatred for men and went from place to place with friends. She would end up back home from time to time, which was hard on her parents. She said about her parents, "Looking back, I know that they did the best that they knew how, because they went through a lot in their lives, too. They were violent, and there was a lot of yelling going on, so it was just a vicious angry cycle inside the home. I look at it as a generational curse that was occurring in my family."

By 18, her former high school friends were graduating and moving forward. She tried having a boyfriend, but her mental state and trauma made it difficult to keep a lasting, healthy relationship. She tried several times, but each time failed.

As Nora increased her drug habit, she was coerced into prostitution through a family who supplied her with drugs. They told her, "Oh, you won't have to do anything," or "Hey, you're going to meet with this guy. He's going to give you some money just to spend time with him." In her naivety, Nora complied and learned another lie of the street life. The first rape multiplied into being raped over and over again. Eventually, she pushed down her feelings and got used to it. She tried to stop; she hated it; and she hated herself.

Nora tried to escape the lifestyle by trying to have a relationship once again, but it did not work out. At 21 years old, she had her first child and lost her boyfriend. She connected with another man that had the same drug addiction and got pregnant again. That time she tried to make it work by going to church and trying to stay off drugs. For eight years, Nora endured a hostile relationship and abuse. She and her boyfriend got hooked on heroin and became homeless together. She lost custody of both of her children.

Nora described, "I ended up on the streets of Over-the-Rhine for 11 years. He left me down there after he was beating me repeatedly, and I kept pressing charges on him. He finally went home. A lot happened down there in the streets. I was in and out of jail a lot. I was beaten and raped a lot. I was forced into prostitution on the streets by a pimp. It was a nightmare. I just had to find ways to survive out there."

To get away from the pimps, Nora would go to the basement of a church in downtown Cincinnati. There she would get food and clean clothes. That is when she met Scarlet in 2010 through Sister Grace and Sarah H., who did art at the Tamar's Program. She got locked up in 2012, and that is when Nora could hear God talking to her and asking her what she was going to do with her life.

When Nora's close friend was murdered, Nora made a deal with God: "Hey, God, next time I get locked up, I'm going to do whatever it takes to stay sober." She got locked up again, but this time, Nora went through treatment at First Step Home. Because of her charges, there were a lot of barriers for her to get housing. She graduated from Drug Court, the First Step Home treatment facility, and then moved into another recovery housing place, Recovery Hotel.

Nora stayed at the Recovery Hotel for three years. While she was there, the girls on the street knew Scarlet and would go to see her; Nora would go with them. Once Nora was sober, Scarlet started mentoring her and became her spiritual advisor.

Said Nora of Scarlet: "She taught me how to pray against foreign spirits. I believe in the principles and principalities and the evil, fiery darts that can come at you. She taught me how to armor up and pray against that. With another lady on the street whom I will call "B," we started going to school together, and I got a job and graduated from Cincinnati State. We had studied at Scarlet's ministry when it was on McMicken Street. We would go there and do our homework, and stuff like that. We started going with Scarlet to worship places. If I had an issue and needed prayer, Scarlet was there for me, and she still is today.

"When I was on the streets, I felt like I was too dirty for God. I just knew that he wouldn't accept me, but now I realize that God was with me the whole time. Now that I'm sober, that is what I reach for. I reach for that feeling of the Holy Spirit, that closeness to God, and wanting to have that deep, close relationship. The closer the relationship with Him that I have, the better I feel."

Nora goes to church with Scarlet at the Church on Fire in Harrison, Ohio. Finally, Nora could feel God coming into her soul and filling that big gaping hole from her childhood. She helps other women, sponsoring girls and doing peer mentoring under the guidance of Scarlet. Nora said, "Scarlet is an amazing woman. She is the general. We call her 'The General' or 'Mama.' She is the front of the line for women to go to. I don't know how she does it. She carries a huge load, and I am very grateful for her. I'm grateful that God placed her in my life so that I can be where I am today."

Scarlet has taken Nora to surgeries; she has served as Nora's power of attorney; and she has filled in the gaps for someone who has lost so much of her childhood and teenage years.

In 2013, Nora made amends with her parents. She has a great relationship with her two daughters and two granddaughters and has a grandson on the way. Nora has just completed her "Certified Peer Support" with the Addiction Counsel Services and is certified through Ohio Chemical Dependency Mental Health Board. She has maintained employment all these years and has gotten a job with a new program, AIM (Afterhours Individual Mobile engagement team), a daytime outreach program. When someone needs services for addiction or treatment or counseling, Nora refers them and takes them.

This year Nora is claiming 2026 as the Year of Jubilee for her. She said, "Regarding men, I have been gifted with forgiveness. It doesn't mean that it's OK what happened to me, but I definitely do not label men like that anymore." She completed a 10-week PTSD therapy, which was helpful to her.

"I learned about forgiveness. I read the Bible. I listen to what the Lord says, and I take it to heart. He forgave me. I sure did a lot of bad stuff myself, but I know that I am at peace today. I really am.

"My dad passed away. My mom is still around. I talk to her every day. She just recovered from a partial mastectomy; she had lung cancer. I made sure that she made it to all of her appointments. She still drinks. She is getting ready to get baptized. I have been praying for healing over my family, my kids, my brothers and sisters.

"My goal is to continue helping others for years to come. Scarlet has such compassion, and now I have it, too."

Prayer Journal of Mama Scar:

7/28/2021

Time to begin again - prayer life must increase, time alone with you must increase. Need to look at what you want of me, not what everyone else is doing.

NO COMPARISON!! STOP IT, GIRL!

Move me, Lord. MOVE ON ME! NEED YOU! I DON'T FEEL ANYTHING - Help me!

I NEED FIRE - LOTS OF FIRE!

Strip me clean, Lord. Create in me a clean heart, one that makes me worthy of your Kingdom! Lord, I AM TIRED OF PLAYING CHURCH!

NO MORE FEAR. I AM A CHILD OF YAHWEH! GLORY TO YAHWEH IN THE HIGHEST, KING OF KINGS, LORD OF LORDS, HOLY IS YOUR NAME! DO NOT TURN YOUR FACE FROM ME. HEAL ME FROM THE INSIDE OUT. PLEASING AND BLAMELESS BEFORE YOU! AND ONLY! MORE OF ME, LORD. DO NOT LET ME LEAVE THE SAME WAY I CAME!

I have been running from You for much too long! Awaken my spirit. Awaken my soul. Deliver me, Lord. Deliver me! Create a clean heart, Oh Lord. Pure and blameless, worthy of your kingdom!

Release a fresh fire, Lord! Fresh fire, Lord. Make me bold, Lord. Bolder than I've ever been, Lord. Fresh fire, Lord!

DO NOT BE AFRAID. STAND FIRM IN THE LORD!

I have a reserve of oil that has not been tapped into yet… Oil will begin to flow when you begin to flow and love on people.

Chapter 12

"God, just take me out."
— Rachel

My schoolgirl friends and I grew up listening to the Beatles. We were 12 years old singing all the lyrics from their Rubber Soul album. The song "Run For Your Life" had a catchy tune, and we would laugh as we emphasized the last syllable from the line, "Catch you with another man, that's the end-DAH, little girl." We were so naive to all the dangers of the world outside of our little group growing up in a private school. As an adult, I still have this melody in my head, but I can no longer sing the unsettling and disturbing lyrics, for example:

"Well, I'd rather see you dead, little girl,

Than to be with another man..."

"Well, you know that I'm a wicked guy..."

"You'd better run for your life if you can, little girl..."

Today, the reality is that there are little girls running for their lives: running from trauma, running from pimps, running from drug pushers, and running from themselves. For Rachel, physically running from a dangerous situation saved her life. She was able to escape physical harm and repeated trauma, but she was not strong enough to escape her drug addiction until she prayed to God for help, and God sent Scarlet.

Rachel is a trim pixie of a girl with remarkably clear blue eyes and a wild mane of black layers of hair scooped from one side to the other over her head and down past her shoulders. Her endearing smile has just the slightest gap between her two front teeth, like Octavia Spencer, Dakota Johnson, and Madonna, which makes one notice her beautiful smile even more. Her black jacket over a white top gave her a classic, yet edgy look. She had a Cyndi Lauper vibe of "Girls Just Want To Have Fun," but fun is not how Rachel would describe her younger years.

Rachel first began drinking in high school and has been an alcoholic her for most of her adult life. She didn't start using drugs until she was in her late 30's. Miraculously with amazing strength, Rachel was able to quit using heroin in 2013; she credits God for removing it from her. However, she would succumb to the alcohol and cocaine repeatedly, mostly because she chose to be around people who were addicts. There was one good friend, Nora, who helped her to make better choices with her life. Nora became her sponsor.

Rachel first met Scarlet when she was delivering food to girls on the street. Rachel started volunteering with the ministry and spending time around the ministry. However, she suffered relapse after relapse. Scarlet took her to many treatment programs; Rachel felt that she had tried everything, including AA (Alcoholics Anonymous) and NA (Narcotics Anonymous). She attributes these failures to not knowing her own worth. As Rachel said, "I was just looking for my worth in worldly things and in a man and in material things. When those things weren't enough for me, I would just fall off again.

"I remember Scarlet telling me one time, 'OK, you've tried everything. Can you just try one more thing?' It was the first building that we had on McMicken Street. I remember being in the office with her, and she said, 'Do you know Jesus?'

"I knew Jesus because I had been raised Catholic, but I was angry at God because of different things in my life: being molested as a child, being raped, losing my best friend to an overdose. I was just mad at God. I felt like, why would he let these things happen?

Scarlet said, 'You know you tried everything else. Let's just try this.' I said the prayer of salvation with her in her office at the first building on McMicken. I remember that it was just right at that moment, all of the things that had happened to me, being molested and all that, all of those things for the first time in my life didn't have a power over me any more. Scarlet allowed me to just sit there and cry and get rid of all of the hurt and anger that I had carried around with me in my life. I felt like for the first time, I felt the first little bit of relief from the feeling of suffocating. Right at that moment, I felt like I could breathe again. I'll never forget that she saved me in her office."

Rachel spent more time with the ministry, and her life started going really well. She was clean for a significant amount of time and was helping with the girls that would come in and help to feed them and get them clothes. She went to Bible study and got baptized, re-baptized in 2018 at Church on Fire by Pastor Doug and Mama Scar.

"I just remember shaking and trembling for hours after that happened. I felt like all of the ugliness was just gone from me. All of the lies from my past were gone from me. I remember them both telling me, 'You have to really be willing to fight now, because the enemy is going to come for you. You have just been baptized, and now you just have to stay on your toes because the enemy is going to come for you.'"

They were right; the enemy continued coming for Rachel. She had been living in a sober living house. She had changed everything in her life, except her boyfriend, who said he was a believer but was not living a clean life. Rachel gave in to the enemy once again.

In her early 40's, yet another "friend" from AA deceived Rachel and kept her locked in his apartment for days. He was selling her for drugs or for money to buy more drugs. He would send guys into a room to do whatever they wanted with her. She was raped repeatedly. While that was happening, Rachel remembers feeling a calmness, like she was outside of herself, looking at herself, thinking, "I know that this is really horrible, but it's going to be OK."

Eventually, Rachel found the courage to escape from the apartment. She knew that the only way out was to wait until someone opened the door, and she would run out. She finally saw the chance and ran out the door past her abuser, who had picked up a knife and was following her. Rachel said, "I just knew he was going to kill me, because he was deranged and not the friend that I thought he had been. He was high on crack cocaine and drinking and had been up for days. He was not the same person that I had been friends with. There was something inside that man that made him deranged."

Rachel had just barely got out the door and was running down Reading Road in Bond Hill with no shoes on. The guy had stopped following her, but she continued running to the underpass of Tennessee Avenue. She never stopped running until she came to a place to be able to call someone to come and get her. She learned that Scarlet or her former boyfriend had filed a missing person report with the police. She went home to her apartment and stayed there, not talking to anyone for weeks.

Eventually, Rachel spoke with Mama Scar. "I felt like the only person that I could tell what happened to me was Mama Scar. I knew that she was the only person that I could tell what happened because she wasn't going to judge me. She wasn't going to blame me, because I felt like everyone was going to blame me."

Scarlet set Rachel up with therapy with Dr. Kelly at the ministry. However, bringing up trauma after trauma and talking about it so much was too much for Rachel. Instead of sharing her level of pain with her therapist, she was secretly still drinking and having horrible PTSD. She sank into deep depression, not caring whether she lived or died.

Finally, in a hotel in Cincinnati, at the Budget Inn, Rachel had a breakthrough. She had been drinking and getting high with people that she had known for quite some time. This time she could see something in those people that she hadn't seen before. She felt as though God was showing her what they really were, and it was evil. Rachel remembers, "It was a dark presence on those individuals that I was with. I just went in the bathroom; I closed the door; and I covered my ears and said to myself, 'God, if this is all there is for me, then please, just take me out. Please end this.'

"At that point, God said, 'Nope. That's not what we're doing. I'm going to send Scarlet again.' Scarlet came down there and she got me and took me home to my daddy out here in the country where I live, where I am from. I had ended up in the city because of things in my life. They put me in the hospital, where I detoxed from the alcohol and the drugs. As soon as I was done with the detox, Scarlet came and got me and took me to her house. She kept me there for a few days. I felt safe. I always feel like she is the only really safe person in my life. She set up the whole thing for me to go to the House of Cherith program in Georgia."

"Truly, I don't remember what happened next, but the next thing I remembered was being on an airplane on my way to the City of Refuge Ministry in Atlanta. It is for women who have been trafficked or sexually exploited in addiction. It is the best thing that ever happened to me, because while I was there, I got a spiritual education. I learned about the things that people can't see. I learned how to fight, not physically, but spiritually. I was fighting a fight that was already won. They put me on a path to getting my education, because I had quit high school. I never got my high school diploma or any of those things. While I was there, I started studying for my high school diploma. It is all because of Scarlet and her ministry.

"It is all because she answers the call, no matter how difficult it is. I know that it has been painful for her to see the things that I've been through and the things that the other girls have been through, but she never said no. She never was not there. She helped me to get my life together. I stayed in Georgia for two years, and when I was done, she drove down and picked me up, and we drove back in less than 24 hours.

"Since then I have gotten my high school diploma, and now I am in nursing school. Everything in my life has changed now because Mama Scar answered the call. When I would call everyone in my family or my friends and ask them to come and help me, they were so sick of me that they wouldn't answer. But Scarlet always answered the call. If it was something that was unreasonable, she would say no, but if it meant to keep me safe or to help me get better, she always answered the call."

Presently at 50 years old, Rachel works in Psych and Addiction as a nursing assistant as she goes to nursing school and works on clinicals. As of January 7, 2025, she is six years clean.

Rachel's daughter had gone to live with her father when she was eight years old, but mother and daughter have reconnected and are working together as nurses in a mental health hospital. Scarlet officiated the daughter's wedding.

Appreciatively, Rachel said: "If Scarlet would not have sent me to Georgia, if she wouldn't have come and taken me out of that hotel, I surely would not be here now in my own home, driving a brand new car, going to school, and making really good money. There are girls that I know who are still out there on the streets, and Mama Scar still shows up for them. They've been out there for 20-30 years, and she still takes them food and still prays with them and still gets them clothes...and she doesn't give up on them. That reminds me of a place in the Bible that the pastor in Georgia shared with me about the prodigal son, not to ever count anyone out because people can always change, no matter what their circumstances are. They can always come back to the Lord."

Because she ran for her life, Rachel is still with us. Because she prayed to God for a way out, Rachel is still alive and sober. Because Scarlet answered her call every time, Rachel is healthy, happy, and helping other people to have a better life.

I can't get those words out of my mind when I think of Rachel's successes. I also can't stop thinking about all those women still on the streets who have not yet been able to escape the chains of addiction and prostitution: I want to say to them, "You'd better run for your life if you can, little girl..."

Prayer Journal of Mama Scar:

4/30/2021

Wake me up, Lord. I am tired and drained. Heal me, Lord. Show me where You are. I don't feel anything anymore. Please help me, Lord. How can I serve You like this? How, Lord? Help me to focus on You, Lord. Help me, Lord. I feel overwhelmed, Lord, completely overwhelmed, over my head, and don't know which way to go. Breathe on me, Lord. Breathe on me, Breath of Yahweh. Holy Spirit, come in POWER and Might!

IN THE MIGHTY NAME OF YESHUA

Chapter 13

"The General" — Scarlet

As the Director of Women of Alabaster, Scarlet Hudson directs the ministry and business of Women of Alabaster. Her skills and duties are many: integrating trauma-informed care to the organization, budget planning and stewardship, vision casting, directing strategic programming, managing donor and relational partnerships. Scarlet also works directly with volunteers, equipping them to serve in the Day Center and on the Street Ministry teams. She is affectionately known by many as "Mama Scar," but to her team of faithful volunteers, she is known as "The General" for her spiritual strength, her clarity of vision, and her ability to mobilize an army in the name of Jesus Christ.

On October 1, 2015, Scarlet launched the first full-time day ministry called Women of Alabaster. Nine years later, on October 1, 2024, I met with Scarlet to plan this book about the ministry, the volunteers, the success stories, and the need for continued support for women suffering from addiction, prostitution, homelessness, poverty, mental illness, and other social ills associated with life in the streets.

When I first met Scarlet, she had heard about Grateful Heart Ministry, which is a retreat house and property that I own and operate with my husband, Darrell. We had acquired property that seemed perfect for pastors, ministers, and other spiritual leaders to find respite, to pray, and to recharge from their exhausting lives in ministry at no charge to them or their organizations. Scarlet indicated that she wanted to reserve a weekend for a celebration for survivor alumni of Women of Alabaster. When I googled the organization, I learned of Scarlet's outreach to sex workers and drug addicts. In my naïveté, I pictured active sex workers and addicts sleeping at the retreat house, and my mind was reeling with too many concerns to verbalize. I wanted to help, I didn't want to be judgmental, but I also didn't want to add worry and extra financial burden that would come with high-risk guests.

I prayed and then called Scarlet personally to tell her that we are not an LLC business nor are we a non-profit organization. We are simply letting others use our house and property while we do all the cleaning and maintenance from our personal family budget. Scarlet said that she understood and really appreciated having a place to celebrate "my girls," as she called them. I had to rely on her incredible open spirit and humbled myself to say, "Can I be honest with you? I don't mind giving women in your ministry a place to rest, pray, and swim. We regularly sanitize the house and bed linens, but we are just concerned with inviting extra "tiny guests" into the house, like bed bugs or fleas or roaches, that would cost us lots of extra money to treat the house and contents for infestations of any sort."

Scarlet quickly helped to ease my mind by explaining that the women were coming to the retreat house with her to celebrate five or more years of recovery, that they were reunited with their families and actively employed in professional jobs. One woman is the CEO of an addiction services organization, one is a phlebotomist, several are working in the food service field, and some work as counselors. As the blush subsided from my face, I apologized to Scarlet for being so short-sighted and paranoid about her women coming to our retreat home. Without being defensive, she said that she understood my reservations and assured me that everyone would be clean and respectful, as well as appreciative. Part of her mission is getting the word out into the communities about the successful women who have been able to break their chains of oppression and find joy in the Lord and in new lives free from their pasts. Every year she invites them to an event to celebrate their continued success in their recovery process.

As a way to show respect to Scarlet, her girls, and their celebration, I wrote individual notes, including a purple heart-shaped stone for them to keep as a tangible sign of their success. I realized that there was so much more to learn about Women of Alabaster and Mama Scar. I searched on the internet and read about their mission, activities, and needs. After their retreat weekend, we received positive feedback from them, and we appreciated their respectful use of the house and grounds.

The next I saw Scarlet, we went to a fundraising event for the Hamilton Dream Center. I told her that I had been writing devotional books. She mentioned that she really needed to write a book about Women of Alabaster. A year later at the same type of event, Scarlet had set up a table to sell coffee mugs and shirts that say, "Leave her alone!" She also had brochures about her ministry. I had set up a table to sell my books. We were seated at the same table for dinner, where Scarlet said that she still wanted to write a book about Women of Alabaster, but she wanted me to write it for her. I was honored and laughed off the idea of my being a ghostwriter for her; however, when her invitation came for a meeting to plan the book, I knew that she was serious about us working together.

I met her in her office at the Hamilton Day Center for Women of Alabaster. It was my first visit there, and I learned that I was not to ghost write, but to write from my perspective about her ministry. I was overwhelmed at the responsibility placed on me to tell her incredible story, but I knew that God calls us and then equips us. We set up several interviews of volunteers, women in recovery, and women still in need of help. Each interview changed my perspectives on street life, but no interview impacted me as much as listening to Scarlet's salvation story and journey in ministry.

Scarlet says that she first met Jesus when she was three years old. While her parents didn't go to church regularly, her father would walk with her or drive her to services at times. She was one of the youngest members of Greenview Baptist Church in Florence, Kentucky, and her grandparents were older members of the same congregation.

By six years old, she was walking to church herself. Back then, six year olds could walk anywhere they wanted without caution, or so she thought, and she always had the desire to be in God's house. However, for Scarlet, the dangers were not from strangers along the streets of Covington. Her danger was closer to her home as a neighbor woman regularly molested her with no one in the family ever knowing. Her mother didn't believe in Jesus and called Scarlet "Goody Two Shoes," but that never deterred Scarlet from believing and loving Jesus.

When she was eight years old, Scarlet's family moved to Covington and went to Epworth Methodist. Scarlet said that God moved with her and moved her away from the abuse. It stopped but she wondered, "Why would God let that happen?" Then she rethought, "He didn't let it happen. Bad things happen to good people, and evil people are out there who have free will, but God was with me. I know that, and I never got mad at him for it. Never."

Another family move took Scarlet to Lookout Heights, Kentucky, to a home where a new church was being constructed behind their house. It was St. Paul United Church of Christ, where Scarlet attended from third to eighth grade.

Scarlet said that her real faith journey started after that.

When Scarlet was in eighth grade, her family moved to Edgewood, Kentucky to Fort Mitchell Baptist Church, and many of Scarlet's friends from school went to that church. She became very active in youth group and on mission trips. She went to Sioux Falls, South Dakota, to work with the children through Vacation Bible School, and to hold a revival. She was the happiest when she was in the house of the Lord. She was baptized on April 13, 1971 at age 13, and her parents came to church that day, which made Scarlet very happy.

Scarlet thinks that her salvation was ever evolving with people of faith walking alongside her and encouraging her, even though at home, it wasn't like that. Her friends' parents were very encouraging and kept telling her, "Keep the faith. Keep the faith."

In her senior year of high school, Scarlet felt a call to become a missionary. However, her calling was diffused. She was conflicted between the spiritual world and her love for home and the natural world. Her pastor, Reverend Taulman, took Scarlet and three other kids to look at Baptist colleges: Cumberland, Campbellsville, and Georgetown. She wanted to go to Georgetown because she felt at peace there. Reverend Taulman said that the church would match the money for tuition since it was a Baptist college. Scarlet wanted to study nursing and social work. For all of her life, she has loved taking care of people.

Meanwhile, home life for Scarlet was difficult. Her father would drink, probably due to his childhood trauma. His mother had left him and his two siblings at an orphanage. She came back to get the other two children, but she left him there. He was nine years old. He had that spirit of rejection on him. He was adopted by a very mean family who abused him for two years before he was taken away from them and given to a couple with strong faith, love, and kindness.

Scarlet's dad fought in the Korean War, met her mom on leave, and shortly after, Scarlet was born. She does not recall how her father served in the war, but it must have been horrific for him. In addition to his abusive childhood and PTSD from war, her father was the product of the generational curse of alcoholism. All of Scarlet's aunts and uncles, with the exception of two, died from alcoholism. Her grandfather was an alcoholic as well.

Regardless of his alcoholism, Scarlet loved her father. She said, "Your dad is the first guy you love. I can remember sitting and watching him shave and smelling Old Spice. I was the oldest, and I had three younger brothers, and he would say, 'Girl, this is no fun!' He was my first love, and I really loved my dad. I loved him a lot. I think that he did the best that he could with what he was capable of, but he was not capable of showing his daughter what it's like to have a Godly man on earth, to have someone to truly love her for just her."

Scarlet went looking for love in all the wrong places. She did not go to Georgetown College, to her parents' dismay. She attended Eastern Kentucky University and "ran wild." She did not graduate. After a year and a half of college, she went home to study at a cosmetology school. Scarlet explained, "I was lost. I went for the drugs; I went for alcohol; and I went for the men. My abuser was a woman, so I didn't like women. My mom was not affectionate. My mom was angry. I think she felt like she deserved better in life.

"My time from leaving Fort Mitchell Baptist, from 18 to 23 years old, was a nightmare. I won't go into any of the details. They are not worth repeating. However, God was still pursuing me. I know that."

When Scarlet was 23, she gave her littlest brother a kidney. Around that same time, she met her husband. His family was everything that hers was not. They were loving. Although they were not attending church, they were strong believers. Scarlet could feel the spirit of God on them. She described them as good, solid people. She could see the fruit of that in their older lives when they began attending church with her in Dillsboro. All her life, Scarlet had wished for a family like that. They loved unconditionally; they did not judge; and they were just happy to see her whenever she could visit. Two years later, she married her husband, and they have been married for 40 years.

Unfortunately, she was still not over her wild spell. For a five year period, her marriage was rocky. He wanted his way; she wanted her way. Scarlet explained, "I continued to drink and to be the party girl. I almost lost him and almost lost our marriage. But God...but God...!"

Two or three years previously, she had gone to a conference and started going to Dillsboro United Methodist Church. She recalls that she was still living in the world but going to church anyway because she knew God. She found herself sitting there and crying, just bawling her eyes out.

At 30 years old, Scarlet and her husband, Bob, were headed for divorce, but God stepped in. Boldly and brashly, Scarlet talked to God, telling Him that when she was done having all her fun, when she turned 50, she would be back. God told her, "OK, little girl. You're not going to get it your way. This is not going to work for you, because I have bigger plans."

Scarlet suffered a nervous breakdown, followed by a hysterectomy, with residual effects that lasted for about ten years. Said Scarlet, "Sin is sin, whether you have excuses for why you did it, it's still a sin against God. I had already given my heart completely to Jesus in 1971, so he's going to get you. He's going to pursue you. He did. For about three or four months, I left my job in the hair industry working for Matrix. I had a good job, made good money, but boy, was I crazy. I couldn't work, couldn't talk, couldn't eat. I had stepped back. I fell backwards, but He never stopped pursuing me."

When Scarlet was 28, she was going to a Methodist church. A woman came to town for a conference and prophesied over Scarlet, "You're going to be taking care of women."

Scarlet responded, "I am not! I don't like 'em!"

She said, "I don't care what you like. The Lord says, 'You're going to take care of women!'"

I said, "Well, we'll see about that."

When she got home, her husband said, "You look different. What happened to you?" She knew then that it was real, that she had had an experience with the Holy Spirit, and it was powerful. For the next six years, she fought God on the idea of helping women. The next time it happened, she was about 35. Actually, she fought God until she turned 57.

She went on a weekend retreat called "Walk to Emmaus." She cried the whole time. During the time called "Dying Moments," she died to her old self and came back a completely different person. She started wearing Jesus T-shirts and trying to get everybody saved. She realized all that she had lost in the interim of walking away from Jesus. All the other hairdressers, who were wild and crazy, asked, "What happened to Scar? Where did she go?" They started to refer to her as the "church lady." She worked Emmaus Walks, went to conferences, and did everything "Jesus" and nothing secular, not even television.

Although her husband wondered about her extreme measures to come back to Jesus, Bob and Scarlet came to a good place in their marriage.

"About 16 years ago, in 2008 or 2009, I started going out with people from my church that did street outreach at the old homeless shelter down on Vine. We'd feed them and then do church with them and do baptisms. Then on Wednesday nights, they went under the bridges on I-75. I went with them. I was doing everything Jesus; I didn't care. I was shocked that under the bridges on I-75, there are whole cities under there. Then they asked me to go out with them on Friday nights with their prostitution ministry. I cried all the way home. God said to me, 'This is what you're going to do.'

"During the next two years, the leaders gravitated toward other ministry positions, and the prostitution ministry stopped momentarily. I was crushed and sat for four months, asking God what to do.

"I thought, 'I can't do this alone.' I had a brand new car, a 2010 beautiful, sporty, teal Escort. The girls kept calling, because they have my phone number. They would say, 'Mama Scarlet, we're hungry. Mama Scarlet, can you take me here? Mama Scarlet, can you take me there?' And that's when it all started.

"I asked Bob if I could quit my job, and he said no. I said, 'Well, ok, then I'm going to do outreach in my brand new car.' I ruined that car. I spilled chili in the back of that car. Bob would make chili for me because I was still working, flying in on Friday. Bob sold his Harley and bought me a van and would have it all set up. He would pack it with all the clothes and food and would make chili and coffee for the girls on Friday nights. Here I would go, down the road with my two outreach partners, Kay and Nicki, and we would hit the streets. Then it just evolved from there. It got to the point of being asked to go to court with them, to go to jail to visit them, etc. It just got to be a lot.

"I told Bob that I really need to open a place on McMicken Street because that was where the girls were.

"Bob said, 'I don't know. Can't you wait until you're 62 when you can get your Social Security?'

"I said, 'Well, I guess.' I wanted to honor him, but it wasn't any time at all before the Lord took me out of my job. I was training sales people, the staff, at our home office. That day God said to anoint the building: the chairs, the walls, the doors, all of it. Anoint it all. The Lord told me to turn on my iPad, to keep it running, and to record everything.

On the first day of training, I remember standing in front of that group and feeling like I was in a bubble, looking out at them. It was demonic. They were saying very cruel things to me on the first day. I really felt the beating, the spiritual warfare, especially from one man in the group. At lunch time, I would just go back to my office to sit and pray instead of eating, asking God, 'What in the world is going on?'

"When I went back in the afternoon, God said to turn my iPad back on. At the end of the first day, I took my iPad home and let my husband listen to it, and he said, 'Where is this man? What hotel is he staying in? I'm going there.'

"I said, 'No, you can't do that.' I was crying and said, I've got to get out of there...' with a few coarse words. Then Bob knew that this was serious. I went in the next day feeling so drained. My boss was going to be in the training that day, so I turned my iPad on again, and she even started attacking me. She wasn't supporting me, and I knew it was as the Bible says that we are not fighting against flesh and blood. I could tell that it was warfare, and I knew why God had me anoint that room and for Bob to anoint me. By lunch time, I was a mess, still feeling like I was in that bubble. When I went into my office and sat down to pray, I heard the Lord say, 'You're done.'

"I said, 'OK, I'm done.' I called Bob to tell him that it was happening again. He said to go in there and finish the day out. Then he said to tell that woman that you're done. God got me out of there. It was hard and weird. I went into my boss's office and recorded our conversation for my husband to hear. God wanted Bob to hear the abuse that I was under.

"She said, 'You can't quit.' I was her director of education.

"I said, 'I'm done.' I said exactly what God said to me and what Bob had said. 'I'll give you two months, sixty days. You will have a standard operating procedure manual, and I have all your shows booked for the spring. But after that, I'm gone.'

"She would keep coming into my office and would lean over my desk and say, 'You can't leave.'

"I said, 'Oh, but I am.' The hair industry had been my career for 32 years, and I was good at what I did. I loved it. It was easy for me, so easy by that point.

"I had been at a substandard company and wasn't trying to climb the ladder, but God didn't want me to. He knew that he was going to pull me out anyway. I was making a really good living. It all seemed like a dream. I'll never forget walking out of there on September 30 and walking into our first Day Center ministry on October 1, 2015 with six years of street ministry under my belt.

"God had told me two years prior to that to pay off all our bills. In March of 2015, I had paid everything off: the house, the cars, the credit cards. It was all gone. I didn't understand it. I didn't know. I wasn't aware enough because I was so busy. My job was very demanding, and I was gone a lot. God definitely orchestrated all of that.

"In that time frame, our chairman of the board of WOA introduced me to a pastor, who was opening a church on McMicken Street. It was a divine appointment.

"After the meeting, the pastor said to the chairman, 'Tell her to come downtown and take a look at the church to see if she wants the ministry to be in the basement.'

"After I had walked through the church on McMicken, I said, 'Yes!' You can just see God's hand all the way through this thing. By October 1, we had gotten it ready. I'd go there after work and on the weekends, and finally, we opened the doors to the girls. It was cold in that basement. I had no money. For almost two years, I ran it on donations that covered the $550 rent a month.

"I shampooed dogs on Saturday for my girlfriend, and I made $100 every Saturday before outreach. I was able to buy groceries, pay for my Obamacare, and put gas in the car. I don't know how we did it. I have no idea. After eight hours of shampooing dogs, I stunk like a dog. When I went to do street outreach at 6:00 on Saturday nights, the girls would say, 'Mom, you smell like wet dog!'

"I said, 'That's because I've been with dogs all day.' The smell was in my hands, but I was so appreciative of my girlfriend, Angela. I will always remember her for giving me that job. God just carried us. There is no reason why we should have made it, other than He knew better than we did. I could budget, and I am not a budgeter. I budgeted that money. I couldn't believe it. And I still could tithe. It was amazing. My story of faith is a long one, and it's never ending. It never ends. I just see God doing all kinds of wonderful things, in spite of me, because I'm definitely like Peter. That is my personality. Let's get it done. Let's go do it. Impulsive. I feel like I'm a visionary. I envision things, like the plan for a farm for the girls that I drew in 2012 at my dining table. I gave it to my friend, a drafter, who put it to scale. That is my goal, wherever He decides, but He knows where I want it."

Scarlet started going to seminary in 2012, but stopped in 2015 when she started the full time ministry. Pastor Pete from her church called her and asked if she wanted to finish school. She did not have the money. He said, "I didn't ask if you had money; I asked if you wanted to finish seminary." The church paid for Scarlet's last two years of school. She wanted to walk for her graduation from Faith Theological Seminary in Tampa, Florida. Pastor Pete and his wife took Scarlet and Bob to Florida for the ceremony and celebration. She became an ordained pastor through Church on Fire in Harrison, Ohio in 2018.

One of Scarlet's favorite Scriptures is from Proverbs.

Rescue those being led away to death; hold back those staggering toward slaughter. If you say, "But we knew nothing about this," does not he who weighs the heart perceive it? Does not he who guards your life know it? Will he not repay everyone according to what they have done?— Proverbs 24:11-12 NIV

Chapter 14

The Significance of the Alabaster Jar: "Leave her alone."

*T*he Prophet Elisha and his counter cultural response to women:
In the second book of Kings, the Old Testament recounts two incidents of the prophet Elisha helping women. In 2 Kings 4:1-7, a widow cries out to Elisha that her husband has died and that her two sons are at risk of being taken as slaves by her husband's creditor. When Elisha asks her what she has in her house, she replies that she has nothing of value, except a small jar of olive oil. Elisha instructs her to ask her neighbors for their empty jars and to fill each jar with oil from her small oil jar and set them aside. The widow complied and her sons complied. Every jar filled with oil, and she was able to sell the oil to pay off her debts, thus redeeming her sons from slavery. She and her sons were able to live off what was left from the sale of the oil.

Immediately following this account is the story of the Shunammite woman in 2 Kings 4: 8-37. After she had provided a place in her home for the prophet Elisha to rest when he came through her city, he asked her what he could do for her. She replied that she was content, that she had a home among her own people. However, Elisha inquired further about her situation and learned from his friend, Gehazi, that the woman had no son. Elisha prophesied over her, saying that she would have a son within a year. She gave birth to a son, who grew and helped his father in the fields. When the son got a headache while working in the fields, his father sent him home, where he died in his mother's arms. Grief stricken, the woman laid her son on Elisha's bed in the prophet's guest room and set off to seek help directly from Elisha.

Despite the objections of her husband to wait until the New Moon or the

Sabbath, the woman set off with a servant in search of Elisha. When she found him, she fell at his feet, crying for his help, despite the objection of Gehazi.

When she reached the man of God at the mountain, she took hold of his feet. Gehazi came over to push her away, but the man of God said, "Leave her alone! She is in bitter distress, but the Lord has hidden it from me and has not told me why." — 2 Kings 4:27 NIV

As the woman informs Elisha of her son's death, he returns home with her and raises her son from the dead.

Elisha summoned Gehazi and said, "Call the Shunammite." And he did. When she came, he said, "Take your son." 37 She came in, fell at his feet and bowed to the ground. Then she took her son and went out. — 2 Kings 4:36 NIV

Once again, the woman is at the feet of the prophet, this time in a posture of thanksgiving for the miracle that he had just performed. He had redeemed her son from the dead.

Consider the significance of these two accounts. Both women cried out to the prophet in their distress and the prophet responded by redeeming their sons for the women. For the first woman, Elisha turns common oil into a rich commodity to sustain her and her family. For the second woman, Elisha allows her to cry at his feet and responds, "Leave her alone!" to the objections of his messenger, Gehazi.

Elisha's life and ministry foreshadow Jesus' ministry with miracles, prophecies, resurrection stories, and judgment against idolatry and religious leaders of the time. Jesus would have been familiar with the Old Testament prophet and the stories of these two women crying out to him for help.

These scenarios are forerunners to the accounts of the women posturing themselves at Jesus' feet. They poured expensive oil from alabaster jars on his head and feet, resulting in the criticism and objections from his disciples. Resonant of the prophet Elisha, Jesus responded, "Leave her alone!" Not only did Jesus defend the women, but he elevated the status of the woman, saying that her action was "a beautiful thing" and memorializing her actions as part of the gospel to be preached around the world. Jesus says, "She did what she could" as a call to action for all to do what we can for the Lord.

In Luke, the woman is described as a sinful woman leading a sinful life, which suggests that she was a prostitute. As she kissed Jesus' feet, cleaned his feet with her tears, and then poured perfume on them, the host Pharisee suggested that Jesus was also unclean by allowing her to touch him at all. Jesus responded by chastising the Pharisees for not washing his feet, kissing him, or anointing his head with oil. Jesus forgave the woman of her sins and saved her by her show of faith. His actions drew further criticism by the guests, questioning who this man was who could forgive sins.

Like the widow in the Bible, the women on the street need a miracle. Their emotional, physical, and spiritual "wounds" need healing. Like the widow's son, the women need Jesus' resurrecting power. As with every person, these women are worthy of being saved and given the chance to transform their lives through a relationship with Christ. Jesus calls the evil in the world to "Leave [them] alone" so that they can respond to His call, shared humbly by the servants of Women of Alabaster.

At the house of Simon the Leper in Bethany - Jesus and an unnamed woman
Gospel of Matthew 26:6-13
6 While Jesus was in Bethany in the home of Simon the Leper, 7 a woman came to him with an alabaster jar of very expensive perfume, which she poured on his head as he was reclining at the table. 8 When the disciples saw this, they were indignant. "Why this waste?" they asked. 9 "This perfume could have been sold at a high price and the money given to the poor." 10 Aware of this, Jesus said to them, "Why are you bothering this woman? She has done a beautiful thing to me. 11 The poor you will always have with you, but you will not always have me. 12 When she poured this perfume on my body, she did it to prepare me for burial. 13 Truly I tell you, wherever this gospel is preached throughout the world, what she has done will also be told, in memory of her." NIV

At the house of Simon the Leper in Bethany - Jesus and an unnamed woman
Gospel of Mark 14:3-9
3 While he was in Bethany, reclining at the table in the home of Simon the Leper, a woman came with an alabaster jar of very expensive perfume, made of pure nard. She broke the jar and poured the perfume on his head.

4 Some of those present were saying indignantly to one another, "Why this waste of perfume? 5 It could have been sold for more than a year's wages and the money given to the poor." And they rebuked her harshly.

6 "Leave her alone," said Jesus. "Why are you bothering her? She has done a beautiful thing to me. 7 The poor you will always have with you, and you can help them any time you want. But you will not always have me. 8 She did what she could. She poured perfume on my body beforehand to prepare for my burial. 9 Truly I tell you, wherever the gospel is preached throughout the world, what she has done will also be told, in memory of her." NIV

At a house of Simon the Pharisee - Jesus and an unnamed "sinful" woman
Gospel of Luke 7:36-50

36 When one of the Pharisees invited Jesus to have dinner with him, he went to the Pharisee's house and reclined at the table. 37 A woman in that town who lived a sinful life learned that Jesus was eating at the Pharisee's house, so she came there with an alabaster jar of perfume. 38 As she stood behind him at his feet weeping, she began to wet his feet with her tears. Then she wiped them with her hair, kissed them and poured perfume on them.

39 When the Pharisee who had invited him saw this, he said to himself, "If this man were a prophet, he would know who is touching him and what kind of woman she is—that she is a sinner."

44 Then he turned toward the woman and said to Simon, "Do you see this woman? I came into your house. You did not give me any water for my feet, but she wet my feet with her tears and wiped them with her hair. 45 You did not give me a kiss, but this woman, from the time I entered, has not stopped kissing my feet. 46 You did not put oil on my head, but she has poured perfume on my feet. 47 Therefore, I tell you, her many sins have been forgiven—as her great love has shown. But whoever has been forgiven little loves little."

48 Then Jesus said to her, "Your sins are forgiven."

49 The other guests began to say among themselves, "Who is this who even forgives sins?"

50 Jesus said to the woman, "Your faith has saved you; go in peace." NIV

At Lazarus' house in Bethany - Jesus and Mary, the sister of Martha (term "alabaster" not mentioned)
Gospel of John 12:1-7

1 Six days before the Passover, Jesus came to Bethany, where Lazarus lived, whom Jesus had raised from the dead. 2 Here a dinner was given in Jesus' honor. Martha served, while Lazarus was among those reclining at the table with him. 3 Then Mary took about a pin of pure nard, an expensive perfume; she poured it on Jesus' feet and wiped his feet with her hair. And the house was filled with the fragrance of the perfume.

4 But one of his disciples, Judas Iscariot, who was later to betray him, objected, 5 "Why wasn't this perfume sold and the money given to the poor? It was worth a year's wages." 6 He did not say this because he cared about the poor but because he was a thief; as keeper of the money bag, he used to help himself to what was put into it.

7 "Leave her alone," Jesus replied. "It was intended that she should save this perfume for the day of my burial. 8 You will always have the poor among you, but you will not always have me." NIV

From the oppression of women in Old and New Testament times to our world today, there is evidence of women crying out and the Lord responding. Sex trafficking, drug addiction, homelessness, abuse, poverty, violence, and repeated trauma are evident in our streets, under our bridges, and in the homes of women (and men) who would not choose any of these conditions for themselves or their children.

Scarlet Hudson is one of our modern day prophets who has the vision, the compassion, and drive to transform the lives of women in crisis in our world. Supporting her is a small army of dedicated volunteers and a few organizations who provide some resources to help. As Scarlet has said, from the first time that she ministered to the women in the streets, she cried all the way home, wondering what she could do to help and how the Lord would call her to action. This is her story, and this book is a call to action. How can we help?

Who are the Women of Alabaster? Who are the women who receive help in the streets and at the day centers? Who are the women who volunteer each week to provide the care and compassion that is needed to run the ministry?

Prayer Journal of Mama Scar:

2/9/2016 - Promise from God

Father God, we come boldly before your throne of Grace and Mercy for those that requested strength tonight, we pray Isaiah 41:10 Fear not, for I am with you, be not dismayed, for I am your God. I will strengthen you. I will help you. I will uphold you with my victorious right hand. NKJV

And Lord, for those crying out for their children tonight; Proverbs 22:6 Train up a child in the way he should go, and when he is old, he will not depart from it.

We stand and agree on this promise, Lord God.

And Lord, for those who need healing in their bodies, Your word says that "by His stripes as are healed" Isaiah 53:5. In Jeremiah 30:17 You say, "But I will restore you to health and heal your wounds, 'because you are called an outcast, Zion for whom no one cares.'" NKJV

And Holy Spirit, we ask for comfort for those who are brokenhearted. Your word says in Psalm 147:3 that you heal the brokenhearted and bind their wounds.

For those, Lord, who are lost and alone, feeling as though they have no one who understands, we pray 1 Peter 5:7 that they cast all their cares upon You, for You care for us. And Psalm 38:9 Lord, all their desires are before You, and their sighing is not hidden from You. NKJV

And Lord God, for those who are recovering from addiction and still trapped there, we pray James 1:12-14 "Blessed is the man who endures temptation; for when he has been approved, he will receive the crown of life which the Lord has promised to those who love Him. Let no one say he is tempted by evil, nor does He Himself tempt anyone. But each one is tempted when he is drawn away by his own desires and enticed (by the enemy of our souls).

And Lord, for those being attacked by the enemy from all sides, we pray James 4:7-8 that they, "therefore submit to God. Resist the devil and he will flee from you. Draw nigh to God and He will draw nigh to you. NKJV

In the name of Jesus Christ of Nazareth, Amen.

Chapter 15

The Significance of "Scarlet"

*I*n the Bible, before Joshua carried out his plan to conquer the city, he sent two spies to scope out the situation. They found refuge and safety in the home of Rahab, a prostitute, whose home was part of the city wall. She hid them on the roof under stalks of flax and lied to the king when he asked her to bring them out from her house. In return for her kindness, Rahab asked the spies to give her a sure sign that she and her entire family would be spared in the siege.

In Joshua Chapter 2, the spies assure Rahab:
14 "Our lives for your lives!" the men assured her. "If you don't tell what we are doing, we will treat you kindly and faithfully when the Lord gives us the land."

17 Now the men had said to her, "This oath you made us swear will not be binding on us 18 unless, when we enter the land, you have tied this scarlet cord in the window through which you let us down, and unless you have brought your father and mother, your brothers and all your family into your house. 19 If any of them go outside your house into the street, their blood will be on their own heads; we will not be responsible. As for those who are in the house with you, their blood will be on our head if a hand is laid on them. 20 But if you tell what we are doing, we will be released from the oath you made us swear."

21 "Agreed," she replied. "Let it be as you say."

So she sent them away, and they departed. And she tied the scarlet cord in the window. NIV

As the account suggests, the city was taken by Joshua and the Israelites, and only Rahab and her entire family were saved. The tangible "sure sign" of Rahab's redemption is the scarlet rope that served two purposes: (1) physical escape to lower the spies and Rahab's family to safety, and (2) a covenant sign of trust and redemption between the Israelites and Rahab's family.

God's plan of redemption was at work well before the spies found refuge in Rahab's home. (1) The spies must have been pure in spirit to be able to enter a home of prostitution with the intent of hiding, and nothing else. They would also have a level of anonymity as strangers likely to enter her house of prostitution. Since her house was part of the city wall (Joshua 2:15), their escape from the city would be faster and easier. (2) Before the spies had arrived, Rahab was already knowledgeable about the conquests of the Israelites and the fear instilled in her people. As a woman of the streets, Rahab would hear the news, the rumors, and the feelings of men from a wide cross section of the city. (3) Rahab was ready to trust the spies because she had already accepted the truth that their God was the God of heaven above and earth below. Her faith in God was just beginning. She would eventually be listed in the family lineage as a direct ancestor of our Redeemer, Jesus Christ. She says the following to the two spies:

Joshua 2:11 *When we heard of it, our hearts melted in fear and everyone's courage failed because of you, for theLord your God is God in heaven above and on the earth below. NIV*

In God's plan of redemption and salvation for humankind, he brought together two polar opposites: the most respected and trustworthy men of his chosen people and the most disrespected and oppressed women of the Gentiles (those who were not Jews). This is early Old Testament evidence that God's plan was to redeem his chosen people of Israel, as well as his "also chosen" people outside the lineage of Abraham, Isaac, and Jacob. During the conquest of Jericho, Rahab assembled all of her family in her house, and the spies saved them and gave them a place to live outside the camp of the Israelites.

Joshua 6:23 *So the young men who had done the spying went in and brought out Rahab, her father and mother, her brothers and sisters and all who belonged to her. They brought out her entire family and put them in a place outside the camp of Israel. NIV*

Joshua 6:25 *But Joshua spared Rahab the prostitute, with her family and all who belonged to her, because she hid the men Joshua had sent as spies to Jericho— and she lives among the Israelites to this day. NIV*

If Rahab and her family were living among the Israelites, her lifestyle would have taken a drastic change as well. She went from a prostitute to becoming the great-great-grandmother of King David, governed under the laws of Israel.

Summarily, the Bible gives evidence that God offers redemption and salvation to all people, and that a prostitute was being used by God, even as she lived outside of the laws of God's people. The prostitute Rahab offered the men protection, and the men subsequently offered her protection and a new life and new lifestyle.

We are all sinners saved by grace, and God uses both saints and sinners in his plan to save his people. Perhaps the most drastic transformation from sinner to saint is the life of Paul. Martyring Christians was his passion until Jesus revealed himself to Paul, who then became one of the most powerful leaders of the church and recognized as the writer of 13 or 14 books of the Bible.

Another example is the Samaritan woman, who had five husbands, yet Jesus revealed himself to her and sent her back to her home to tell people that he was the Messiah. From sinner to saved, she became the first evangelist for Christ.

The Biblical story of Rahab and the scarlet rope resonates with people who are working in the streets today. There are prostitutes and often homeless women who must rely on men especially for their daily and dangerous existence. Also in the streets today are teams of Christian women and men who go to the prostitutes, addicts, and homeless to bring them food, clothing, blankets, kind words, hugs, and lots of prayer. The women are offered an escape from their dangerous lifestyles and existence if they are willing to get the help provided. Scarlet Hudson and her team throw a lifeline of safety and salvation, which is similar to the scarlet rope over the wall of Jericho as a symbol of safety, trust, and redemption. The scarlet rope of Scripture helped to save a prostitute and her entire family, as well as the spies and their people. Scarlet and her volunteers work to save prostitutes and their entire families from the cycle of poverty, oppression, addiction, and violence. Her name, Scarlet, is spiritually tied to Scripture. Her nickname, "Mama Scar," is physically tied to the scars she and her women carry that share the pain of their stories. Jesus' restorative work in their lives is what has brought beauty to those scars.

Chapter 16

"Grace, Grit, and the Power of Being Seen" — Lisa Mertz

"**B**y the time I stood at the podium as valedictorian of my law school class, I had already lived a dozen lifetimes. My story isn't just one of recovery—it is resurrection. Though I first met Mama Scarlet while working in the jail, I wasn't searching for God at the time. I wanted nothing to do with faith, but something deeper stirred. I found myself drawn to the Women of Alabaster Ministry—not by pressure, but by presence. I began volunteering, quietly following the woman who would one day become my second mother. Then, one day in a street outreach van, everything changed. I broke down in tears and whispered, 'I need Jesus.'

"The women of the ministry stayed with me, prayed with me, and welcomed me home. Mama baptized me, mentored me, and helped me walk into the calling I never imagined I was worthy of. My valedictory speech marks a moment of triumph shaped by years of grace, grit, and the quiet power of being seen."

The Valedictory of Lisa Mertz
NKU Chase College of Law

Good evening, everyone.

It is the honor of a lifetime to stand here as the valedictorian of the part-time evening division. A group that—let's be honest—often feels like the lost children of law school. We work full-time, raise families, attend night classes, and keep Red Bull in business. And yet, somehow, we made it.

But if you had told me a little over a decade ago that I'd be standing here, in cap and gown, I would've laughed... or cried... or both. You see, about ten years ago, I was homeless, battling severe alcoholism and addiction, and thought my story was over. I had lost everything.

But then... everything changed. A local treatment center took me in. I lived in transitional housing for a year and began to rebuild—one step at a time.

Along the way, I met people who saw something in me before I could see it in myself.

Judge Melba Marsh—who is here tonight—was one of the first. She didn't see a case file; she saw a human being with potential. That changed everything.

And then there was Charmaine McGuffey—then a Major in the jail, now Hamilton County's Sheriff—who let me volunteer in the jail when I didn't think I had any value at all. She told me, "When the world says no, that means go." And I did. I went.

Little did I know that- one day-she'd be writing my law school recommendation letter.

Eventually, I began working as a recovery coach at a local treatment center. I never could have imagined that one day, I'd be leading an organization like the Addiction Services Council as its CEO.

Still, law school seemed like a fantasy. I mean, I've wanted to be a lawyer since I was a weird 8-year-old, watching Perry Mason reruns on loop while other kids were watching cartoons.

But getting into law school after everything I'd been through? That was hard. I had a lot of history—about 250 pages of disclosures, to be exact. And when I got to the part asking for ten years of past addresses, I didn't know what to write—there's no checkbox for "homeless." I felt so defeated when I hit submit. I thought, they're never going to accept me.

But once again, people believed in me. The Chase admissions committee said yes—to me. Baggage and all.

That first year? I had a full-blown case of imposter syndrome. I thought people would judge me. But instead, they embraced me.

Gracie was the first to know my past. She didn't flinch. She celebrated me. Gabi, Jessica, Mia—you made me feel like I belonged. Hunter—my unofficial CALI rival—you made me better. (Even though I still think I deserved that Con Law award. We can talk about that later.)

Leigh—when I first met you, I said I didn't like cops. You said, "I'm not like most cops." And you weren't lying. You are one of the most compassionate and hardworking women I know. And now, I'm proud to call this cop my friend.

Even our professors went above and beyond. Professor Kreder—when I had a hard breakup and my spark dimmed, you noticed. You checked in. You were ready to use your Marriott points to make sure I had a safe place to sleep. Who does that? Only at Chase.

And to Professor Graham: I'm convinced your UCC final shaved years off my life. I saw the Uniform Commercial Code in my dreams—for weeks.

And Professor Nacev, you told me the VITA tax clinic would count for pro bono hours. You didn't mention it was a lifetime sentence. I'll be doing taxes in the afterlife.

Tonight, I probably have the biggest crew to ever show up for a law school graduation—from people in the recovery community... to my colleagues at the Addiction Services Council, who are my slightly dysfunctional second family... to the staff of the Hamilton County Justice Center and court system, who have worked alongside me to advocate for recovery in criminal justice... to the women who've walked beside me in sobriety—especially my best friend Nicole, who has never left my side... and to Mama Scarlet, Pastor and leader of the Women of Alabaster Ministry, and all the women from that ministry who stood by me and helped me build a relationship with God.

To my children, Joel and Brooke—you are the light of my life. To my mom— thank you for giving me grace I didn't deserve and never giving up on me. You believed in me before I did.

Look around this room. Every background—race, gender, sexual orientation, culture, and faith—is represented in my support system, and I wouldn't have it any other way. I didn't get here alone. I am a product of second chances. I worked hard, yes—but I also had an army.

Class of 2025: You will be lawyers, judges, lawmakers, and policymakers. Please remember—some of the most brilliant people you'll meet won't wear suits. They might be sitting in jail cells. Or struggling to survive.

I came to law school to fight for those voices, and after seeing the grace and strength in this graduating class, I know we're going to change the world.

Wherever you go, remember the underserved. Remember the people who weren't invited into rooms like this. Use your voice to lift theirs.

I worked hard to earn this JD—but I stand here because my community gave me the chance to.

Thank you. Thank you for seeing me. And thank you for letting me be exactly who I am.

"Redemption rarely happens all at once. It unfolds in unlikely places—courtrooms, jail cells, outreach vans, and sanctuaries made of folding chairs and faithful women. The Women of Alabaster Ministry didn't just witness my transformation—they walked it with me. Today, I am called to lead a major recovery organization, to fight for justice, and to lift up the voices of the forgotten. More than that, I am living out the very heart of the ministry: that no one is beyond reach, and no story is beyond hope."

Afterword

𝓛eave

by K.P.
(one of Mama's girls)
2025

This morning I awoke clutching your
name with such reckless devotion
that it turned into dust

I know how I found you

guided by the lessons in the shadows
of my mistakes

You were there in my deepest and
darkest moments of despair

I was lost and thought I could never
be found.

Then I heard a voice and my
knees hit the ground

I yelled screamed and pleaded

And you said,

There there child for I am all
that you've needed

I've been there the whole time
you've cried.

Come on, love, let's take another
toke

You gave all your time to me
finally alone at last.

Come on, baby, let's take another
blast

Remember when you didn't have me
and I showed you the way

The way to sell your body and
how to get paid

'Cause that's where I tricked you. I
made you think my time had to
be bought

When real time is priceless and
with me can never really be
got

It can never be got held or
obtained

It is merely a facade made to
make you insane.

My time with you for now
seems over.

If you want more fun time
you're always welcome to come
over.

K.P. 2025

107

Time
(written by one of Mama's girls)

I have all the time in the
world for you

Actually, I have time now
Let's go get a cold brew

That's it. That's how we will
start the night.

We can reminisce on all the
fun we had.

I was even there when you
lost your dad.

Remember all the time we
spent

That night so cold in our little
tent.

Or how about the day your
grandma passed away

You gave me purpose and hope

Watched you self-destruct and weep
As your loved ones died.

When you loved that glass thing more
than me

Still my love right there would
always be

Hidden of the shadows or the
lessons I bestowed

It wasn't a shadow of shame
But simply where I heard you
Call my name

It was that moment when I
allowed you, God, to enter my heart

The moment I knew I could never
be left or allow myself to fall
apart

K.P. 2025

All proceeds of this book support Women of Alabaster
To donate or to learn more: www.womenofalabaster.org

To schedule Scarlet Hudson and others for speaking engagements:
scarlet@womenofalabaster.org

To speak to Scarlet:
513-543-5656

To send donation by check written to "Women of Alabaster":
7716 Arlington Rd. Dillsboro, IN 47018

Appendix I: Women of Alabaster & Social Media Excerpts

https://www.womenofalabaster.org/
https://www.facebook.com/womenofalabaster.org

GET EDUCATED. GET INVOLVED. WHAT WE KNOW ABOUT HUMAN TRAFFICKING

According to the United States Justice Department, 83% of victims in confirmed sex trafficking incidents were identified as US citizens. Sex trafficking is a $32 billion dollar industry, a market-driven industry that operates on the principles of supply and demand. A pimp can make $150,000-$200,000, and the average pimp has 4-6 girls. Girls as young as 5 years old have been trafficked and sold into child prostitution. The average age for entering sex trafficking is 15, and for boys, it's even younger. Low self esteem and need for love, acceptance, and understanding is a vulnerability that traffickers prey upon. Traffickers often target people who are poor, vulnerable, living in an unsafe situation, or searching for a better life.

FACEBOOK POST MAY 17, 2023

A WORD FROM MAMA SCAR:

This week has been an emotional week for our teams. At the day centers, there were too many moments of watching the girls struggle through the chaos. At the jails, we witnessed our sweet girls sharing pent-up feelings and emotions.

BUT GOD...

In the past two weeks, 6 women were baptized in Butler and Hamilton County Jail taking the next step with Jesus. Another surrendered to a program and we are praying this will be the last time.

Yesterday, during the one-on-one pastoral care at Butler County Jail, our sweet "T" shared she was going to prison for 6 years, and she didn't want me to forget her, not like I ever could. Then she went back to her cell and came out with this precious bracelet. She made them out of her plastic rosary, and string from her blanket and clothing!! I was and still am wrecked by her thoughtfulness. She gave out of what she had and what was in her hands.

The love of God is so tangible and so powerful. Please pray for the ministry. Pray that the Lord continues to order our steps each day and that we give Him our best yes.

Day Ministry, Outreach, and Jail Volunteers, you make a difference feeding, clothing, nursing wounds and most importantly praying and loving like Christ.

Thanks for being the hands and feet of Christ.

Matthew 25:36-37 Jesus says, "I was naked and you gave me clothing, I was sick and you took care of me, I was in prison and you visited me."

FACEBOOK POST DECEMBER 28, 2023
Dearest of Friends,

We have yet again lost another of our precious ones on Monday.

Theresa is and will always be such a light, she will continue to live in our hearts and minds. She found so much joy in the simple things and she was always so appreciative of everything that you all provided for her. Know this: she accepted Jesus as her Savior, and she was doing the best she could at this time. And now she is completely free and all things are made new. She finally has what she always desired, her Home in Heaven. Rest in Peace My Sweet Daughter...I will Forever Miss You! Love Always, Mama Scar

FACEBOOK POST FROM SCARLET ON APRIL 31, 2024
My thoughts today from Chicago! It was an honor to serve Grace Ministry and Chicago Dream Center Team the last couple days for their outreach ministry and strip club ministry. God opened doors for learning into a new level of understanding the need for the Holy Spirit to lead and direct as they minister on the streets. I might be trying to figure out what's going on but ...I Am Gifted and My anointing is for an appointed time.

FACEBOOK POST JUNE 28, 2024
Arts and crafts provide a non-threatening way to have casual conversations that often lead to deeper truths. When we provide creative outlets, we provide an escape from reality and a reason for our friends to find pride in themselves.

NAOMI'S STORY:
My name is Naomi and I have been a user for 14 years of heroin, fentanyl, and whatever they're cutting it with. My arms are being eaten away; it's a flesh eating disease and it doesn't go away. It gets worse, and it's down to the bone before I got into the hospital. I just hope that people will catch it in the beginning and not let it get as far as I did. I have no movement in my arms; I can't stretch them out all the way. I can't open my hands all the way. I don't know if my arms will ever be the same. I'm not losing them right now, and I hope I don't. I don't want to see anybody lose their arms. Hopefully, if I reach out to at least one person... I definitely appreciate all the prayers from everyone, from Mama Scarlet and Lisa, and just everyone. And all these nurses here at Good Sam, I got good nurses. If there's any hospital you should go to, it's Good Sam, because they're

going to treat you the best. Every other hospital, I've been forced out or treated like sh*t. You know, my pain wasn't addressed because I was an addict, and it's not fair to have to suffer in pain. You don't have to. Good Samaritan Hospital will treat you right and treat your pain and thank you to everybody that prays for me. I love you guys.

Facebook Post July 9, 2024
Living fully free and completely healed doesn't happen overnight. The scars and trauma of sex trafficking and addiction remain long after the physical chains have been removed. That's why Women of Alabaster remain in relationship with our survivor friends for the long haul.

Women of Alabaster continue to support, encourage and love our friends by providing them with purposeful care. In addition to friendly check-ins and conversations, we have scheduled monthly dinners and devotions. And this month, we'll host our annual survivor retreat, "Freedom Weekend." Freedom Weekend allows our alumni (survivors) to connect with one another and lose themselves in the beauty of creation and the goodness of the Creator.

Facebook Post July 20, 2024
The next time you see her, pause on the judgment. You don't know her story. You don't know how badly she wants freedom. You don't know all she's already done to get free. You also don't understand the Father's love for her.

Facebook Post July 24, 2024
Do you know what it's like to be homeless? Have you ever slept in a run-off tunnel leading to the river, and then a huge rain comes and washes you into the river, leaving your body bruised and cut? Have you ever left your home, and settled in another state, to have someone take advantage of you because they knew you were scared and desperate for shelter?

Thanks to collaboration with TLC, Transitional Living Consultants, we have acquired apartments at the YWCA for 3 of our sweet sisters. These apartments are furnished with everything our friends need to live happily and free from fearful nights on the street.

Facebook Post July 24, 2024
POUR IT OUT FRIEND
One of our guests sat at the craft table first thing this morning. Asked her if she wanted clothes or food. She said she really wanted to paint what was on her heart. Her focus and determination are so intentional, what a beautiful soul "A" is! Pray she finds her way to freedom soon....until then we will be here to shepherd her through.

Facebook Post July 25, 2024
The fight for our victimized friends is intense. Daily the battle reveals a field of victims and casualties that is bigger than us. We know God is with us and for

us. We trust in that 100%. Yet, we need others to join the battle.

We know that only some are called to walk on the battlefield. However, would you join the battle by resourcing the battle? Would you please consider giving it today? No gift is too small and every gift is useful for the war.

Here are just some of the ways your gift could strengthen the WOA mission:

- Provide gas to get a precious soul to recovery or the hospital.
- Secure the transportation ticket that gets a victim of trafficking back home.
- Provides a dignified way of laying to rest God's fallen child.

Today, would you consider joining the army by giving?

FACEBOOK POST AUGUST 7, 2024

A rescue took place tonight, thanks to our dedicated WOA Warriors who bring ministry to the streets. Thanks to their efforts, a young girl is now off the streets and safely tucked in bed tonight. We're thanking God we were where we needed to be. We'd also like to thank those who support WOA. Your giving makes it possible for nights like this. We did this together!

FACEBOOK POST AUGUST 8, 2024: RECOVERY BOUND!

Nina has decided it was time to reclaim her life and she chose a program in Atlanta that will enable her to thrive in her personal life and grow in faith. Before she headed out, the WOA Warriors bathed her with prayer and affirmation. We sent her off wearing the love of many hugs and the promise of many prayers. Would you join us in praying for her?

Pray that nothing would get in the way of all the LORD has for her. Thank you for giving. Your giving supplied the Greyhound Bus ticket that carried her to her new life.

Would you please join the mission by partnering with us financially?

FACEBOOK POST AUGUST 14, 2024

Once a week, our vulnerable friends can visit our day center's Agape Clothing Room to select one outfit that consists of a shirt, pants, underwear, bra, socks, and a jacket. Due to their life on the streets, we do not receive the items back. This leads to a constant need for clothing donations.

In about a month's time, we gave away 1000 items JUST from our Downtown Cincinnati day center!!!! At this time we are completely out of underwear and socks/footies. Could you help us restock our supplies?

To make your shopping easier, check out our WIsh Lists on Amazon. The Summer List contains the items we have urgent need for now. Thank you for anything you can do.

FACEBOOK POST SEPTEMBER 22, 2024

My career of 32 years was making people beautiful! I loved watching the sheer joy on the faces of the hundreds of clients who sat in my chair. There is no greater honor than giving a first haircut and then the very important cut for first grade, the prom and ultimately the wedding. I've heard stories of joy, loss and the heartbreak of losing a loved one. But now we get to make special 'Daughters of the King' celebrate life for a brief moment to feel beautiful!

My prayer for each of them as they look in the mirror and see the time lost to the life so many live each day., Is a brief encounter with the King of Kings and Our Lord Jesus. And the beauties they are to Him and us who get to serve them. With a braid, haircut, make-up, a shower, clean clothes and a hot meal. You, my sweet girls, are beautiful and lovely. We Love You All! Mama Scar

MAMA SCAR'S NIGHT DRIVE HOME:
I just wanted to share with you that tonight we had four baptisms this weekend, two in Hamilton County Jail and two tonight at Butler County Jail. God is moving, and every single girl tonight raised her hand for salvation, so God is on the move and quickly moving. I believe that we are going to see a greater coming to the Lord from those that are lost and broken. I am going to ask you to increase your prayers for all those who are in jails, in prisons, trapped on the streets. They are so important to God, and there is an urgency there. We are in a time of great revival. I believe that God wants to do things in us and through us as God's people. I encourage you to stand up, to stand up for Jesus. There is no man that is going to save us, only Jesus. It is Jesus that we are waiting for; it is Jesus that we are waiting to see; it is Jesus that we are wanting. I don't want anybody to be left. I just want everyone to come home to Jesus.

I get really encouraged by these nights to keep doing what we're doing. I had a strong team tonight, Rebecca and Amy and Gina, this afternoon with Miss Karen, Miss Shawna, and we are seeing a great move of God inside the jails. Tonight at Butler County Jail, we had 17 women to minister to today. God just keeps bringing them, and I think that if we keep opening our hearts and doors to them, God will keep bringing more.

When you go to the store, look for somebody to pray for. When you're driving your car, pray for the person you are driving past that they would find Jesus. Just lift up the name of Jesus, the Lord of lords and King of kings. You can tell that I am a little emotional tonight. Join me in praying Psalm 91 (God is my Refuge and my Fortress) over and over again. Pray for me. I'm a little under the weather. I'm going home to bed. Thank you for your prayers. God bless you, and God bless the REC Team (Residents Encounter Christ) going into Jennings County tomorrow for a three-day weekend. Bless them going into the Jennings County Jail that will bring the love of Christ and for those who will experience, many for the first time, the love of Christ. I pray that they will be strengthened in their resolve for the Lord, and that the team will stay healthy and strong for the Lord. I pray that the men they served last weekend and the women that they will serve this weekend will come to know Christ as their Lord and Savior.

FACEBOOK POST: REPORT FROM HAMILTON CHRISTIAN CENTER OUTREACH

We got to serve some amazing women a meal, sit with them, pray over them while some get to move into a home after being homeless, another made a life changing decision, so we pray for protection and strength for her. This organization provides a place for women to come in off the street, get a hot meal, clean clothes, shower, sleep and guidance both spiritual and personal. If your organization or you yourself are looking for an organization to spend some time with, please consider spending some time here. I promise it's life changing for the women you help and for you. Thank you to Momma Scar, Tammy and Leah for all you do and allowing us to be a small portion of your village today. We pray God continues to bless your ministry and the work you do, We pray he continues to protect you and your women. We look forward to being part of your village. It truly is an honor.

FACEBOOK POST FROM PATRIOTS OF AMERICA

Scarlet Hudson of Women of Alabaster made a special trip to Illinois to witness on the streets and to assist in mentoring our team on trafficking. Thank you, Scarlet, as you are a true warrior for Christ.

The Lord did some amazing things over the last couple nights. We prayed with many women including their pimps who walked up to us while we prayed with the women....We went through dozens of sandwiches, cases of water and other donated items these women need while on the streets. One man walked up to our van before we hit the streets and asked for prayer and accepted Christ as his Lord and Savior. Many of these women who we see on the streets week after week are expressing to us how tired they are and just a day closer to the time they say, "Let's go. Take me." God has sent the resources our way for these women (victims on the streets) and when they are ready we will be there.

Our team could use the community's help with items while out there.... Water, sanitizer wipes, tooth brushes, tampons, gift cards for the sandwiches we provide and gas cards for travel expenses. Donated items are much needed. There's many things you can do to help fight this fight of sex trafficking without hitting the streets with us. PM me for more info on how you can help with donation items.

FACEBOOK POST SEPTEMBER 25, 2024

Recently, we had the honor of having nursing students from ATA College serve at our Hamilton and Downtown Cincinnati Day Centers. The knowledge they gained will assist them in becoming outstanding nurses. Listen to what they had to say about their experience.

"Being there, I felt a mix of emotions-compassion, sadness, and hope. It was hard not to be moved by the stories of hardship and resilience that these women shared. Many had been through unimaginable trauma, yet there they were, taking steps toward recovery and a better life. I learned that the journey to recovery is not just about addressing physical needs, but also about providing emotional support, building trust, and restoring a sense of self-worth. The women I met taught me about the importance of empathy, patience and the power of supportive community. This facility is a testament to the fact that with the right support, even those who have faced the darkest of times can find a path to healing and hope."

FACEBOOK POST SEPTEMBER 28, 2024

The WOA day centers are more than centers to care for trafficked victims. Beyond providing the basic needs that life on the streets can't provide, they provide a place where victims can come to be with family. They are a family at Women of Alabaster. They laugh together. They cry together. They stand with each other and they celebrate together.

This past Thursday I (Anita Ridener) paid a visit to Hamilton Day Center. I always love my visits to the centers. This past visit reminded me why I love the visits. There is something beautiful about a place that offers rest and escape for every wounded soul that walks through its doors.

What do the weary experience? Hugs, lots of hugs. Sweet words of greeting, lots of sweet words. They find warm beds, showers, clothes, and hot food. They find hope for the day and tomorrow. They find an abundance of affirmation that communicates they matter to everyone at WOA but more importantly to God.

How do these lovelies respond? They love back! They genuinely care for each other and those who serve at WOA. They notice when a "sister" is struggling. They pray for each other. They celebrate milestones such as birthdays and victories.

One such victory was shared as this sweetie got her hair cut. From under her long locks, you heard "twenty-seven days!" For twenty-seven days she has been clean!! A few minutes later another sweetie asked Mama for prayer because she was sick from addiction and would soon begin working through a recovery program. The center came to a stop, and everyone there surrounded her to pray because that's what family does.

Appendix II: Scarlet's Prayer Journal Excerpts 2015-2023

INTERCESSION (1)
- Learned from Holy Spirit
- Not us putting our burdens on God for another
- God putting the burdens on us for another
- Hear the heart of God for lost, hurting & burdened
- We may not know what to pray but the Spirit does through us to accomplish the will of the Father
- Holy Spirit must pray for us. He knows the needs & every condition of every person
- We must surrender our hearts and words to Him - so Holy Spirit prays in us & through us

INTERCESSION (2)
- Nothing is accomplished without prayer
- God effects His will on earth through prayers of His Saints Matt 6:5-18; 18:19-20
- Holy Spirit, help me to pray for others even when I have no idea how to pray for their needs.

Get in the War Room before the Battle
- Battles are often lost before the first engagement
- Develop a strategy
- Decisions are made to reveal the Victor Jesus + US!

Set my mind with Holy Spirit realities not earthly ones

Colossians 2:1:
If then you were raised with Christ, seek those things which are above, where Christ is sitting at the right hand of God.

—

2-12-2016

Dear God, Hear our prayer of thanksgiving tonight for the healing of our sister of breast cancer. We prayed and You are the God that heals. Your Word tells us to arise and go our way, that our faith has made us well. Luke 17:11-19. Also, Lord, for the visible miracle of healing today at the conference, for eye sight restored. We give You all the praise, honor, and glory. For the impartation of knowledge of things seen and unseen. We "'Bless the Lord, O my (our) soul(s), And forget not all His benefits" Psalm 103:2 NKJV

Prayer for forgiveness. Lord Jesus, you made it clear when You said, "And when you stand praying, if you hold anything against anyone, forgive him, so that your Father in heaven may forgive you your sins. Mark 11:25. Father, if anyone is holding a grudge for past hurts in their heart tonight, we ask that they let it go right now, confess, repent, and forgive. In Jesus' Name.

Jesus, we lift up the unsaved tonight. 2 Corinthians 4:4 tells us it is "the god of this world (the devil) hath blinded the minds of them which believe not, lest the light of the glorious gospel of Christ, who is the image of God, should shine unto them." God, You are not willing that (Name of loved one) perish, but that they come to repentance. 2 Peter 3:9. It is Your Will that my loved one be saved and comes to a knowledge of truth. 1 Timothy 2:4. We believed that ALL our household will be saved. Acts 16:31. We bind on this earth the strongmen keeping our loved one from being saved, and I loose salvation on earth and in the heavenly realm on our loved one's behalf. Matthew 18:18

Hear our request for wisdom, Lord God, in ALL situations. In Proverbs 4:6-7 You tell us not to forsake wisdom, and she will protect you; love her, and she will watch over you. That the beginning of wisdom is this; get wisdom, though it costs all you have, get understanding. To the person who pleases Him, God gives wisdom, knowledge, and happiness, but to the sinner, he gives the task of gathering and storing up wrath to hand it over to the one who pleases God. Ecc. 2:26

Lord, for those going out to serve Your people on the streets tomorrow night, we pray we do Your Will in ALL encounters. The people are crying for You, Lord. Anoint us like You did Benjamin, and send us to these lost and broken as spiritual captains over Your people, that they might be saved out of the hand of the enemy. 1 Samuel 9:16. You have anointed us and delivered us from the hands of our enemies, just as You did King David. 2 Samuel 12:7.

Hear our prayer, Lord God. Praise and Thank You.
In the name of Jesus Christ of Nazareth, Amen.

2/18/2016   PRAY THE WORD

Lord, hear our prayer tonight for strength, wisdom, understanding, and peace. Your Word tells us to not be anxious for anything, but in every situation, by prayer and petition, with thanksgiving, present our request to You, God. (Phil. 4:6) We believe Your Word and we know You are not a God that You should lie. So, tonight, we stand on that Word for all those suffering from cancer. Your Word says as it is in Heaven, it shall be on earth. We believe we are completely healed in Heaven and also that is Your will for us here. So, tonight we decree and declare, according to Job 22:28 that healing is taking lace right now, in Jesus' Name.

There are those tonight thirsting for a drink from the Water of Life; Your Word says, I (we) thirst; therefore, I (we) come to You, oh God, and drink that Living Water (John 7:37). With joy, Lord God, we draw healing water out of the wells of salvation (Isa. 12:3). And we believe the healing of the Lord will spring forth speedily (Isa. 58:8). We are crying out to You, God, and You heal us. You have kept us alive (Ps. 30:2-3) for by Your stripes we are healed! Isa. 53:5

Lord, tonight Your people are burdened with broken relationships, someone has spoken words of hurt and actions so painful over their brothers and sisters, but You, Lord, are able to repair, redeem and restore us and mend our hearts, minds, and souls. Help us to find the strength to forgive and then to move on. If we are the offender, Lord, help us to humble ourselves, offer forgiveness and have patience during the process. Your Word tells us to be humble, gentle, and patient. Show Your love by being tolerant with one another (Eph. 4:2) and to be kind and tender hearted to one another, as You, God, forgave us through Christ. (Eph. 4:32) Your Word says, Lord, that you are near to the broken hearted and You save those who are crushed in Spirit. (Psalm 34:18). We trust You, Lord, to bring peace in this time of distress.

For those who have lost their way, we ask that they confess, repent, and walk in the newness of light. We thank You for Your tender mercy and grace, assuring us of Your unconditional love for us.

Lord, tonight we thank You for bringing home lost children. You are our shield and strength; our hearts trust in You, and You helped the families of those who have been lost and are now home once again. (Psalm 28:7) And for those still out there, we pray tonight that You place someone in their path to point them home.

In Jesus Christ of Nazareth's Name,
Amen.

———

3/16/2016   PRAY THE WORD AGAINST SUICIDAL THOUGHTS
Lord Father, we come to You tonight on behalf of (name). We first bind the spirit of suicide and loose the power of the Lord Jesus Christ over (name)'s mind. Your Word tells (name) to "Fear not, for You are with (name), that she should not be dismayed, for You are her God; You will strengthen her. You will help her. You will uphold her with Your righteous right hand." Therefore, any assignment against her life is nullified by You and the enemy has NO FURTHER HOLD ON HER MIND. (Isaiah 41:10)

Psalm 34:17-20
When she, her parents and prayer intercessors pray, You hear the righteous cry for help. You hear and deliver (name) out of her troubles. You are near to her brokenheartedness and You save her crushed spirit. Many are the afflictions of the righteous, but the Lord delivers (name) out of the affliction of suicidal thoughts. You keep all her bones and not one of them will be broken.

Jeremiah 29:11
Lord, You are fighting for (name), and You know the plans You have for her. You declare those plans through Your Word, plans for her good and not for evil, to give her a future and a hope.

1 Cor. 6:15
Her body is the temple of the Holy Spirit within her, whom she has from God. She is not her own but Yours. Therefore, the enemy has NO LEGAL RIGHT to her, according to Your Word!

John 10:10
It says in Your Word that the thief comes to kill, steal, and destroy, but You came that she may have life and have it more abundantly. Therefore, (name) will not die, but she shall live, and recount the deeds of You, her Lord.

1 John 4:1
We, as intercessors, Lord, do not believe this suicide spirit, because we have tested it and know it is not from God. It is false and is therefore gone from her now, in Jesus' Name. We cry out tonight on her behalf and stand together as one, a wall of fire around her, calling down 10,000 angels to encamp round about her. And You, oh God, will supply her every need according to Your riches in glory in Christ Jesus.

Now the Lord is the Spirit, and where the Spirit of the Lord is, there is freedom.

In Jesus Christ of Nazareth's Name. Amen.

Habakkuk 2:2-4
> *'Then the Lord answered me and said: "Write the vision And make it plain on tablets, That he may run who reads it. For the vision is yet for an appointed time; But at the end it will speak, and it will not lie. Though it tarries, wait for it; Because it will surely come, It will not tarry. "Behold the proud, His soul is not upright in him; But the just shall live by his faith.'*
> *NKJV*

Remove any obstacles that stand in the way of a life lived out with you in the lives of these women. I pray for complete healing. Yeshua, help me to know how to serve you and to serve those you place in front of me. I place my trust and confidence in you. Show me the way back to Yahweh, Yeshua, Holy Spirit. Blessings, Love, Lord. Amen.

—

1/2020 PRAYER FOR THE FARM
- Anointing of farm, staff, ministry
- Funding - lead and guide us and those who will support these women
- Lead us to those who will be coming to be ministered to, open their eyes and hearts to receive you, Lord

- Volunteers who will bring the Holy Spirit to lead, guide, and direct
- Open hearts to receive us into the community
- Churches that will come alongside to share the gospel
- Make the vision clear, give us wisdom and knowledge as we move into this new place of ministry
- Lord, minister to the hearts and minds of those who will be serving these women.

—

IT IS NOT FINISHED 8/2

I am the Lord and I say when you have completed your assignment. Listen and hear my voice. Be obedient in all seasons. When I call, be quick to respond. Do not even linger for one second. I am coming soon! Be ready for the hour is close. Few hear my voice. Tell them of me; show them my love. Do not miss one of mine, I am in front of you! Don't hesitate - release my glory on the people - don't hold back. Please do it now! My children are dying without me. The longer you wait, the more are lost. Be diligent. Fight for them. I breathed life in you; breathe on your brothers and sisters. Do it now. LIsten to the words I speak.

Day Ministry
- Salvations for each woman and man who enter the building
- Decisions to leave the life
- Supernatural appointments for each person who enters
- Believing volunteers with the strength of a Heavenly Spiritual Army
- Support for each area of ministry
- Unity in spirit, vision, and mission
- Each day we meet our assignments with joy and complete them with excellence
- Bring Esther's, Deborah's, Mary's, Esther's, Naomi's

—

3/18/2020

Dear Lord,

Today, I praise and bless you, for You are holy and You alone are worth. Come, Lord Jesus, stand in the gap for Your people. Holy Spirit, be at work in my life. You have full reign over me. Help me to be faithful to the end. I will not let what's happening in this world change my love and faith. I consecrate the first of the day, the entire light hour, and as I sleep, come to me and speak to me of what you would have me to do. Do not ever stop speaking to me. Lord, help me to be open to the leading and guiding of the Holy Spirit. Be in my heart and be in my mind. Control my whole being. Cover me, Lord, with the complete gospel message. Do not let me wait but be eager in all seasons to carry the full gospel message to those you chose. Change my heart, move in and completely encompass my mind, body, and spirit.

Please do not let one area of my life not be changed by you. But transform me, Lord, transform me. Check all my motives and thoughts. Come, Lord Jesus, come. Be thou magnified and glorified always in my life. Help me be more like you and less like the world. Holy are You, Oh Lord. Holy Holy Holy

—

7/1/2020
Dear Lord, This year is running by. So many things are happening that are making me angry, bitter, and frustrated. Change my heart, Lord. Renew a right spirit in me. Each day when I rise, give me your joy and peace and mercy. Help me to bring all of me that is good into the day. Lord, create a clean heart in me. Help me to sow peace, love and revival into this land.

Yahweh, it feels so evil at times here on earth and I see people saying they want a better life, but they are destroying your creation. I pray each of their souls be cleansed and replaced with You, Lord. Come, Yeshua, do what only you and the Holy Spirit can do. Show me, Yahweh, what it is I am to do. Heal our land, Lord. Heal our land.

—

11/10/2020   HABAKKUK 2
Prayer for Peace - waiting and watching in the midnight hour. Nations be healed in the mighty name of Yeshua! Do not hide your face from us, Lord, from me, Lord.

You, Oh Lord, have awakened my spirit. It was dead and now is alive. I will be bold for you, Oh Lord. You have loved me with an everlasting love. I will trust your unfailing love! Your Word, Yahweh, gives me life, true life. No weapon formed against me will prosper. Be bold, my child, proclaim the goodness of Yahweh. Thank you for this time apart from the world. You have placed me in a peculiar place to grow and bloom. It's time for me to preach the gospel to the people, a true Word given by You. Keep me steady. I am focusing on You. Awaken my Spirit. Hear my cry. It's you, Lord, only. Deliver me from the snare of the fowler. I trust in You alone. Remember your time in Israel in the garden, mind at peace - I walked where You, Yeshua, walked on the Sea of Galilee, arms outstretched to You, Yahweh - standing on the shore knowing You walked on water there. I KNEW YOU WERE THERE in the quiet. Forgive for missing You in that place.

—

1/29/2022
You are here, Lord, in the midst of us, loving us, healing us. Glory is shining all around You, Lord. Your daughters hear Your voice and answer You beckoning. Beckon us, Oh Lord. We are in Your Holy Holy Presence, Lord. We are so in awe of You, oh Lord. Most Holy Lord, Most Holy Lord. - Change us, Lord.

2/1/2022

The Lord is getting the Big Farm ready - more will come in Jesus' Name.
You don't want to be dazzled with the spectacular - you want to be comfortable with the supernatural.

★ Yahweh sharpen my senses - fix my gaze on the unseen realm
Refresh a move of Yahweh in my life, Holy Spirit!

Lord, speak, speak to me and give me revelation only You can impart - vision of You

Take me away from this world to my Heavenly Home, Lord, where You and my Savior are. Holy Spirit, reveal all you have to teach me. Help me, Lord. Help me to hear only Your voice.I REPENT FOR ALL I HAVE DONE AGAINST YOU AND YOUR PEOPLE, LORD. For anyone I have hurt, help me, Lord. I have not served You well, Lord. Forgive me. Search me, Lord!

—

2/27/2022

Lord, You are taking me to the next season with You. something has changed and I am hungry for Your voice, Your smell, Your presence, Lord. Just to be with You, just You and me alone in the secret place. A new understanding, a new revelation, a prophetic trail. I am here waiting to see You clearer, brighter, stronger, and lifted up powerful and mighty, first and foremost, You are the first and the last of my day. Nothing can come between us.

Activation:
- STOP PRAY AM & PM Deut. 6:4-5
- Listen for instruction
- Bring petitions to Him
- Go to the Word for instruction
- Worship Him, praise Him, invite Him
- Enter into relationship with Him and ask His opinion before asking others
- Look for His hand to direct you throughout the day, if you become frustrated or confused (STOP-PRAY-LISTEN-MOVE FORWARD)

BIG ASK: **ARE YOU**?
Matt 22 But Jesus answered and said, "You do not know what you ask. Are you able to drink the cup that I am about to drink, and be baptized with the baptism that I am baptized with?" They said to Him, "WE ARE ABLE."

BIG QUESTION: **WILL WE**?
Matt 23 So He said to them, "You will indeed drink My cup, and be baptized with the baptism that I am baptized with; but to sit on My right hand and on my left is not Mine to give, but it is for those for whom it is prepared by My Father."

Father, help me today to be worthy to sit at Your feet. To worship and praise You for all You have done. To honor Yeshua and to be in the Presence of Holiness. Make me, Lord, into the unlikely vessel. I AM UNDONE!!

John 12:27:

> *"Now my soul is troubled, and what shall I say? "Father, save me from this hour?" But for this purpose I came to this hour."*

When my soul is troubled and I beg for help, I will remember this verse. You are my comforter, Holy Spirit. I WILL REST IN YOU!

—

4/25/2022 ANNA HOUR

Pour out your oil, God, on us tonight. Let us see, hear, and taste Your Glory, Lord. Bring us into a new dimension where you are tangible. Help us to reach a higher place of encounter with You, Lord. Bring us into the Kingdom where the Throne illuminates Your Glory. We want to go higher, Lord. Bring us, Lord, into the place of shalom, Lord.

—

August 27, 2022

> Healing is in the peace of the Lord
> Revelation is in the peace of the Lord
> Wisdom is in the peace of the Lord
> Knowledge is in the intimacy with the Lord

I have an appointed time - the Lord wants to release you to do greater things. He says can I trust you with more. What are you doing with what I have given you...is there fruit in what you hold for me? Are you doing all unto me, if not, why? What are you afraid of or who are you afraid of, men or Me? What is it going to take for you to release from your hands the anointing placed there. Your anointing was bought and paid for by My Son on the cross of Calvary. All was laid bare there. You are and were made Holy that very day.

Why don't you just come up here and sit with me awhile. Let me put a fresh fire in you. Come now. Don't hesitate. Just trust me and come. There is so much more I want to show you and tell you about. I need you to hurry now. Don't tarry. Don't wait and please don't hesitate. I am here always, but I need you to come now. It's urgent. I have time with you NOW! Are you coming.....?

Keep Walking

Appendix III: WOA Vision, Mission, & Ministry Team Values

WOMEN OF ALABASTER MINISTRY, INC.

Our Mission:
To provide a pathway to freedom for vulnerable women who are victims of sex trafficking and addiction.

Our Vision:
To re-build their self respect and self worth, to renew their faith in human kindness, and to restore their desire for a life of victory.

Women of Alabaster came into existence when Scarlet Hudson, founder and director of Women of Alabaster, volunteered to go out with her church to serve 'prostitutes'. That evening, Scarlet found herself hiding behind a hotel with a pistol whipped prostitute. She did not know that this encounter would change the course of many lives, her own and those in need of help. God soon revealed to Scarlet that she was to leave her prestigious career and care for the vulnerable and victimized on the streets.

Women of Alabaster, Inc. was launched in 2012. We are a 501-C3 faith-based organization. We reach for those whose vulnerabilities make them easy prey for the sex trafficking industry. We care for those who have already experienced the horror and pain of sexual trafficking and addiction. We are a presence in forgotten communities and a voice for those that society so easily discards.

Women of Alabaster 2025 Standard Operating Procedure Manual

Core Values:
Everything centers around relationship with God, ourselves, and others.

Values for ministry team members:
1. Be a born again believer in Jesus Christ (John 3:3)
2. Be a part of a local church (Hebrews 10:25)
3. Attend all ministry training sessions (Philippians 4:13)

A Ministry Team member must demonstrate the following:
1. Humility (James 4:6, 1 Peter 5:5)
2. Obedience (1 Samuel 15:22)
3. Submissive (James 4:7, Ephesians 5:21)
4. A Teachable Spirit (1 Timothy 2:2, 15)

5. The Fruit of the Spirit (Galatians 5:22-25)
6. No prejudice (Revelation 7:9)
7. Walking in Forgiveness (Ephesians 4:30-31)
8. Have a consistent prayer life (1 Thessalonians 5:17)
9. Daily study the word of God (2 Timothy 2:15)
10. Faithfulness (1 Corinthians 4:2)
11. A servant's heart (John 13:1-16)
12. A calling from God to serve in this capacity (Matthew 4:18-22)
13. Peer recognition as a Godly Person (1 Thessalonians 5:12)
14. LIving a Godly lifestyle (Titus 2:11-12)

Woman of Alabaster Team Covenant

To surrender my "Self" to the power of Christ at work in me; to live my life as one with Christ; and to so order my life that the love of Christ will be visible and inspire other team members and the Women of Alabaster.

- To follow the example of Christ in servanthood and humility.
- To pray for the women and men before and after outreach.
- To set aside my own theology, agendas, views and thoughts, to completely empty me of me so Christ can be seen and revealed.
- To be willing to listen and learn and to be taught by the "Women of Alabaster" leaders and by the Spirit of Christ.
- To remember that this outreach is not for me but for the women and men we come to serve.
- That my role during outreach is as one with the other servants, and my service is no more important than any other.
- The team member shall give evidence of a genuine experience of salvation, and also give evidence of a consistent Christian life.
- The manner in which things are done is often more important than the things themselves.
- It is inevitable that occasions will arise that will try your faith. If, on that occasion, the team member becomes exasperated, harsh or critical, the results of his attitude could be damaging to self, others, and to this ministry. Courtesy, love, patience, longsuffering, and other Christ-like traits come from the heart. One needs a Christ-like heart to meet the problems with a Christ-like spirit.
- The team member must be willing to learn. No two people are alike. It takes patience and effort to understand people. No two outreaches will be exactly the same.
- The team member must learn to adapt themselves to new situations. Only through God's help, a careful study of people, readiness to adjust to circumstances, and a determination to improve his or her technique, will the team member reach the peak of their effectiveness.
- The team member must maintain a proper devotional life. One of the dangers of those who deal with spiritual things is that holy things become

commonplace. One of the best safeguards against danger is to maintain a consistent "Biblical" devotional life.

Signed: _____

Date: _____

Outreach Leader: _____

I can do all things through Christ Jesus who gives me strength. Philippians 4:13

Related Scriptures

Exodus 22:20-26: *God will hear the cry of the poor and vulnerable, and they should not be oppressed.*

Leviticus 19:9-10: *"A portion of the harvest should be set aside for the poor and strangers."*

Isaiah 58:6-7: *"Is not this the fast that I choose: to loose the bonds of wickedness, to undo the straps of the yoke, to let the oppressed go free, and to break every yoke? Is it not to share your bread with the hungry and bring the homeless poor into your house; when you see the naked, to cover him, and not to hide yourself from your own flesh?" NKJV*

Isaiah 61:1: *"The Spirit of the Lord God is upon me, because the Lord has anointed me to bring good news to the poor; he has sent me to bind up the brokenhearted, to proclaim liberty to the captives, and the opening of the prison to those who are bound;"*

Ezekiel 34:16: *"I will seek the lost, and I will bring back the strayed, and I will bind up the injured, and I will strengthen the weak, and the fat and the strong I will destroy. I will feed them in justice."*

Zechariah 7:10: *"Do not oppress the widow, the fatherless, the sojourner, or the poor, and let none of you devise evil against another in your heart."*

Proverbs 31:8-9: *"Open your mouth for the mute, for the rights of all who are destitute. Open your mouth, judge righteously, defend the rights of the poor and needy."*

Proverbs 14:31: *Oppressing the poor is a serious offense, and a sin against God.*

Psalm 35:10: *"All my bones shall say, "O Lord, who is like you, delivering the poor from him who is too strong for him, the poor and needy from him who robs him?"*

Psalm 68:5-6: *"Father of the fatherless and protector of widows is God in his holy habitation. God settles the solitary in a home; he leads out the prisoners to prosperity, but the rebellious dwell in a parched land."*

Psalm 82:3: *"Give justice to the weak and the fatherless; maintain the right of the afflicted and the destitute."*

Psalm 82:4: *"Rescue the weak and the needy; deliver them from the hand of the wicked."*

Psalm 140:12: *"The Lord maintains the cause of the afflicted and executes justice for the needy."*

Psalm 146:9: *"The Lord watches over the sojourners; he upholds the widow and the fatherless, but the way of the wicked he brings to ruin."*

Matthew 25:40: *"And the King will answer them, 'Truly, I say to you, as you did it to one of the least of these my brothers, you did it to me.'"*

Luke 4:18-19: *"The Spirit of the Lord is upon me, because he has anointed me to proclaim good news to the poor. He has sent me to proclaim liberty to the captives and recovering of sight to the blind, to set at liberty those who are oppressed, to proclaim the year of the Lord's favor."*

Luke 12:33-34: *"Possessions should be sold and given to the poor, and a treasure in heaven should be provided."*

John 10:10: *"The thief comes only to steal and kill and destroy. I came that they may have life and have it abundantly."*

Romans 8:15: *"For you did not receive the spirit of slavery to fall back into fear, but you have received the Spirit of adoption as sons, by whom we cry, 'Abba! Father!'"*

Ephesians 1:4-5: *"Even as he chose us in him before the foundation of the world, that we should be holy and blameless before him. In love he predestined us for adoption to himself as sons through Jesus Christ, according to the purpose of his will,"*

All proceeds of this book support Women of Alabaster
To donate or to learn more: www.womenofalabaster.org

To schedule Scarlet Hudson and others for speaking engagements:
scarlet@womenofalabaster.org

To speak to Scarlet:
513-543-5656

To send donation by check written to "Women of Alabaster":
7716 Arlington Rd. Dillsboro, IN 47018

Thank you in advance!